Praise for *In a Land of Awe: Finding Reverence in the Search for Wild Horses*

"*In a Land of Awe* is the author's voyage of discovery—part poetry, part history, part philosophy, part adventure. Wild horses are transformative, and Chad Hanson describes how they transformed him from avid cyclist and fly fisherman to wild horse watcher, admirer, and advocate. So beautifully written it will transport the reader, as it did for this wild horse lover."

—Ginger Kathrens, founder of the Cloud Foundation, Emmy Award-winning filmmaker, wild horse adopter, and documentarian

"Chad Hanson has written a wonderful book exploring his fascination with the wild horses of the American West, taking readers on a journey inside the lives of these magnificent animals and the wild places where they still live. Weaving together sociology, ecology, and history, Hanson explores the importance of a reverence for nature to human psychology, why wild horses inspire awe, and why saving them is essential to preserving the last vestiges of all that is wild in the West. An excellent read!"

—Suzanne Roy, executive director, American Wild Horse Campaign

"Chad Hanson brings us into his encounters with wild horses so that we may examine the value of wildness in our lives, and the immense crater that will remain if it disappears. This examination of why and how wild horses enrich our society and our souls makes us consider what is really important."

—Carol J. Walker, author of *Wild Hoofbeats: America's Vanishing Wild Horses*

"Tearfully delicate and deeply sincere, *In a Land of Awe* paints a lyrical portrait of what it feels like to experience the rich textures of the American West. It's a journey story that naturally intertwines the nuances of the issues it explores. Not only will readers be inspired to care; they'll be compelled to go out into nature in search of wonder and wild horses."

—Ashley Avis, founder of Winterstone Pictures, president of the Wild Beauty Foundation, and writer/director of Disney's *Black Beauty*

"Hanson sets out to find the soul of the American West, through the majesty of open spaces and the magic of the wild horses that inhabit them. *In a Land of Awe* takes the reader on a journey through the human psyche and through enigmatic Western landscapes, with lyrical storytelling peppered with penetrating insights. A page-turner."

—Eric Molvar, author and conservation professional

"*In a Land of Awe* offers a close look at the mysterious and fascinating world of wild horses. Walk with Chad Hanson on this journey. Find truth, beauty, and maybe even yourself on the way."

—Clare Staples, founder and president, Skydog Ranch & Sanctuary

"Horses are amazingly sensitive sentient beings. Chad Hanson's beautifully written and highly personal *In a Land of Awe* does an outstanding job of informing readers about the awe-inspiring lives of wild horses in the West: their families and their futures. Readers will come away feeling deeply connected or reconnected with horses and their homes."

—Marc Bekoff, PhD, author of *Rewilding Our Hearts: Building Pathways of Compassion and Coexistence* and *A Dog's World: Imagining the Lives of Dogs in a World without Humans*

IN A LAND OF AWE

Also by Chad Hanson

Nonfiction

Trout Streams of the Heart
Swimming with Trout

Poetry

This Human Shape
Patches of Light

Scholarship

In Search of Self: Exploring Student Identity Development (Editor)
The Community College and the Good Society

IN A LAND OF AWE

Finding Reverence
in the Search
for Wild Horses

BY CHAD HANSON

BROADLEAF BOOKS
MINNEAPOLIS

IN A LAND OF AWE
Finding Reverence in the Search for Wild Horses

Except from "The Wild Divine" is taken from *Bright Dead Things* by Ada Limon (Minneapolis: Milkweed Editions, 2015). Copyright (c) 2015 by Ada Limon. Reprinted with permission from Milkweed Editions. milkweed.org

Cover design: Cindy Laun

Print ISBN: 978-1-5064-8219-4
eBook ISBN: 978-1-5064-8220-0

For Tuffy …

… and in memory
of Lara Joy Brynildssen.

No synonym for God is so perfect as beauty.

—John Muir

Horses make a landscape look more beautiful.

—Alice Walker

CONTENTS

PROLOGUE:
LANDSCAPES WITH WILD HORSES

The sea, the woods, the mountains, all suffer in comparison with the prairie . . . the prairie has a stronger hold upon the senses. Its sublimity arises from its unbounded extent . . . its calm, self-confident grandeur . . . its power of throwing a man back upon himself.

—Albert Pike, *Journeys in the Prairie*

My god is the horse.

—common saying among the Mandan people

I lived in Wyoming for a decade before I learned that the state hosts sixteen herds of wild horses. I didn't move to the West for the mustangs or the plains, however. I moved for the mountains and the trout. The state of Wyoming is a fly fisher's paradise. Free-flowing streams roll down from glacier-studded peaks. Then the waters move through forests and in between the walls of rock canyons. The state's rivers have furnished the setting for countless stories and magazine advertisements. They also provide clients for the shops and outfitters that line our downtown streets.

I am like everybody else. I moved to the West for the backpacking, fly fishing, and other high-country adventures. Then, one morning, while driving a stretch of dry prairie with my wife, Lynn, I noticed a band of wild horses through the window of the car.

I don't fish for trout much anymore.

Until I saw them in front of me, I assumed that wild horses were part of our past. I pictured them as the sort of thing that schoolkids read about in books. I placed mustangs in a mental category next to unicorns, and that is where they stayed until—by chance—as a way to avoid high wind and hail on a westbound interstate, Lynn and I took a detour through the Great Divide Basin. We were rushing along, trying to find a way out of a storm, and there they were. I remember crouching in the grass with my eyes locked on them. I watched their behavior toward one another, and I thought about how they fit on the land, between bunches of sage. There's only one way to describe my feeling: "Awe."

As part of the research for her book *The Nature Fix*, Florence Williams interviewed Paul Piff, a psychologist at the University of California. According to Piff, awe is something that "blows your mind" in a literal, biochemical sense. In the nineteenth century, both Ralph Waldo Emerson and Henry David Thoreau pointed out, and scientists confirm today, nature provides the most likely setting for feelings of reverence. Think of a waterfall, a shooting star, or a flock of sandhill cranes so big the birds block the light from the sun. Picture a band of wild mustangs running on a ridge. Such sights provide us with occasions to transcend.

Of late, researchers who focus on the relationship between people and nature have turned their attention to the particular effect of awe-inspiring encounters. The consensus is that feelings of wonderment or veneration tend to move us deep into a moment, to a place where a sense of humility rises to our awareness. Awe-inspired people describe a diminished sense of their own importance. Feelings of spirituality often spring from the experience. Studies also confirm that feelings of awe lead to increased levels of goodwill, generosity, an increased ability to exercise patience, and an orientation to the collective interests of human beings as a group.

Emily Esfahani Smith conducted a review of the literature on awe in preparation for her 2017 book *The Power of Meaning*. In the studies that Esfahani Smith examined, investigators presented people with images of mountain peaks, cathedrals, inspirational music, and examples of moral courage. Across the new lines of research, analysts found their subjects poised to make statements such as "I am part of the universe" and "I am part of humanity."

Until now, generations of psychologists have described moments that lead to feelings of awe as examples of "peak" events with recognizable qualities. In one of the earliest and more telling statements on the subject, Abraham Maslow suggests, "it is quite characteristic in peak experiences that the whole universe is perceived as an integrated and unified whole." He continues by explaining how the perception that "the universe is all of a piece and that one has a place in it … can be so profound and shaking that it can change a person's character." As he clarifies the point, Maslow comes to a conclusion: "Practically everything that happens in peak experiences, naturalistic though they are, could be listed under the heading of religious happenings."

Similarly, in the age before research caught up with the musings of philosophers, William James imagined much of what we know today with regard to feelings of awe. In his 1902 text,

The Varieties of Religious Experience, James explains, "Religious rapture, moral enthusiasm … cosmic emotion … all are unifying states of mind, in which the sand and grit of selfhood are inclined to disappear, and tenderness to rule."

The death of the ego.
A growing sense of widespread unity.
The cultivation of feelings of kindness toward others and the world.

Moments of contact with the nonhuman hold the potential to move us in these directions. For example, in *The Radiant Lives of Animals*, the Chickasaw novelist and poet Linda Hogan describes how feelings of veneration accompany her in time spent among horses. For Hogan, the act of watching a horse inspires feelings of reverence, in part, because horses possess "different kinds of knowledge and different ways of knowing." She explains, "In the traditional worldview, we have awe of them."

For the rabbi and theologian Abraham Joshua Heschel, "Awe is the beginning of wisdom." Feelings of immensity force a change in the way our brains function. Ordinarily, in our culture, we spend time using our minds to measure, take stock, and evaluate. From kindergarten to college, our schools teach us to speak and think in the language of calculation. As a result, when we look out onto our landscapes, we tend to see bushels-per-acre, tonnage of ore, barrels of oil, and acre-feet of water. It often takes a moment of awe to shift us away from calculations toward something more akin to contemplation.

I am trained in sociology and anthropology. Scholars in both fields aim their efforts at one basic question: "Why?" Social scientists look for patterns in life or behavior. When we find one, we ask, "Why?" and then we go to work attempting to explain. After I saw my first band of mustangs, it started to feel like I had come under a spell. I wanted to know why I felt so compelled to spend time in the presence of wild horses. I needed to identify the spring that fed the roots of my inclination, so I did what a social scientist would. I went to the library.

There, I discovered a whole body of horse literature: history, lore, genetics, and a series of books on equine therapy—a technique for using horses to heal our unseen wounds. I discovered evidence that time spent with horses can lessen the impact of post-traumatic stress. It also turns out that children with autism show signs of improvement after interacting with the animals. In the past, horses carried warriors into battle. They plowed our fields. They still serve as our companions, and to this day we gather in stadiums to watch them try to outrun each other. For a variety of reasons, we either tend toward horses for their services or we find ourselves caught in the grip of their allure.

Paleontologists point out that the horse and humankind evolved from one common "stem animal." If you backtrack the lines of evolution, you eventually reach a point where our predecessors turn into the same creature. We share 87 percent of our DNA with *Equus caballus*. The logo of the American Museum of Natural History once included an image of two skeletons side by side, a horse and man—the horse standing on its hind legs and the man alongside the beast. The similarities stoke the imagination. Arms and legs. Two spines and matching rib cages. The horse looks like a big person.

With respect to our minds, horses and humans also share a good deal. Evolutionary biologists describe how the social relations among people provided the need for our cognitive skills to grow. The most important part of that process involved the development of our talent with words. We learned to use language in order to navigate our relationships.

Horses are social, too. Perhaps even more so than us. Wild mustangs live in families or bands comparable to ours. Stallions and mares engage in rituals of courtship, not unlike our own. They use physical touch to show affection and build bonds of trust. When foals are born, the adults in a family each play a role in raising the young. Unattached bachelor stallions often lurk beside established bands with the hope of gaining the attention of a mare. On occasion it works. Clusters of bachelors also come together, forming groups. They spend their days teasing each other and practicing for a time when they can begin new families of their own. Sometimes, when I watch bands of wild horses, it feels like a soap opera, plots unfolding through a range of motion, storylines set to a silent score of theme music.

Across time, and all over the surface of the earth, humanity created languages. In contrast, horses shifted their communication in the direction of touch. They became tactile. On the steppes of the West, I watch them nibble and nuzzle each other. Adult horses coddle their young. Both mares and stallions stand over the bodies of sleeping foals to protect them. Then they'll give them a nudge when it is time to rise. If foals try to sleep in past the end of their nap, an adult will add a whinny and a hoof to lift their head. They see the world through a lens much like our own, but a human life is different in that it unfolds in a web of words.

Humans use narratives to give meaning to our existence. If a part of your life involves spending time with wild horses, you will likely begin giving names to them, and they'll turn into characters. You will weave the experience into a story, one that you can tell yourself and then retell. Our experiences, and our recollections afterward, hold deep seats in our minds. Each occurrence becomes a point, placed upon a longer spectrum, that we then assemble into life stories. In *Orlando*, Virginia Woolf describes memory as the "seamstress" who threads our lives together.

Wild horses and prairies did not become a part of my story until after I turned forty. My interest in ski slopes, mountain bikes, and fly fishing kept me from seeing the grandeur in a large part of the West. At this stage of life, however, I've had the experience of witnessing bands of mustangs run, eat, sleep, play, fight, and care for each other. I can attest: Wild horses on a landscape summon the attention. Their presence can create moments that stand outside of time. Watching them forces you to cultivate a unique kind of presence to the beauty of the world. "Beauty is sacred. Beauty is lifesaving," writes the philosopher Elaine Scarry. She goes on to suggest that beauty "incites deliberation," and in her book *On Beauty and Being* Scarry explains how something beautiful "fills the mind yet invites the search for something beyond itself, something larger."

Prettiness alone rarely moves us all the way to captivation or immersion, however. It's more often hallowed places that rise up to claim our thoughts at a level where we are left changed when we come down on the other side. For the Buddhists who practice in the Pure Land tradition, it is the sight of Mount Lu in China that produces the kind of absorption we associate with reverie. In Pure Land Buddhism, practitioners hold the belief that proper living leads to rebirth in the Pure Land—a place of calm and radiance—a place where enlightenment becomes more attainable than we find in the here and now. Days, months, or even years spent in the shadow of Mount Lu can provide a Buddhist with meaning and a route to progress on the path.

For the Christian Celts of ancient Europe, it was the heaths, or highlands—rolling fields of flowing grass—that offered steps toward transcendence. Such places bear a striking similarity to the prairies of the western United States. The Celts crafted the phrase "thin places" to describe geographies that blend the physical with the sacred. Celtic folklore has it that "heaven and earth are only three feet apart," but in a thin place, "that distance is smaller." Krista Tippett defines thin places in the book *Becoming Wise*. She describes them as "places and times where the veil between heaven and earth, between temporal and eternal is worn thin." Others have described such places as permeable, places where one might find a rip in the fabric of the air, allowing passage from the everyday to the rarified.

Thin places have been felt and sighted in different locales: coastal regions, riversides, and mountaintops. In the case of streams and oceans, it's the magic of water that rouses feelings of mysticism. Rivers run and waves crash on the shore. Bodies of water offer movement and in the case of clear water, a chance to see inside the element that animates our own bodies. With regard to mountains, it's the aesthetic of a ridgeline, and the proximity to the heavens that inspire.

Still, it was the European version of our high plains first identified as a thin place. A walk onto the chaparral is something inimitable. It's consolidating. When you walk on the prairie you find an earth and sky sandwich—you in the middle—the self in the center where it merges with the world. It's a big canvas, one that makes it possible to live more fully than you find in other surroundings. In *The Varieties of Religious Experience*, William James includes the words of Charles Kingsley on the topic of time spent in open spaces: "When I walk the fields, I am oppressed now and then with an innate feeling that everything I see has meaning, if I could but understand it. And this feeling of being surrounded with truths which I cannot grasp amounts to indescribable awe."

Of course, there is no guarantee that a walk on the grasslands will stir something that borders on the spiritual. In *Becoming Wise*, Tippett portrays the short-lived and passing nature of thin places. She describes the experience by suggesting, in the right time and location, "our senses take in a different kind of reality," but only in "snatches that come like gifts." Then she goes on to convey the value of the gift that a thin place can provide. She explains how time spent in the proper setting can "send us back with a lighter step, and yet more passionately engaged in ordinary life."

As a testimony to that effect, in a letter to a friend, the novelist Sherwood Anderson ponders a chapter of his past: "I can remember old fellows in my hometown speaking freely of an evening spent on the big empty plains." He describes how "it had taken the shrillness out of them." He claims, "They had learned the trick of quiet," and he tells his friend that the old men had developed "a sense of bigness outside of themselves." At the end of the letter, he wonders, "Has that been lost?"

Here in the twenty-first century, I share Anderson's concern that our sense of bigness has been lost. My hope is that public grasslands and wild horses can become a larger part of the American experience. In my first encounter with a band of mustangs, I could feel myself seeking with my senses. I found myself leaning out to the edges of my mind's capacity. I want my nieces and nephews to have that experience. I want my students to have it. I want my neighbors and their families to have it too. I want us to find ourselves locked in contemplative encounters, in the presence of some of the last examples of full-sized, free-roaming megafauna left on this good continent. I want us to be able to pause, reflect, and let the memories fold themselves into our stories. I want us to tell and retell those tales until they start to teach us what to value.

Sometimes I wonder, who would we become as a people if sage-covered prairies with wild horses running on them were the landscapes of our memory? If we could possess them in that way, wouldn't they also come to possess us as well? If memories of wild horses and prairies were what made us, then in some way, wouldn't we become them? Over the years, the rolling grasslands of the West have come to occupy a large space in my mind, a space that I return to for replenishment and awe. Near the middle of my life story I discovered, if you wander the prairie long enough, the prairie starts to wander you. In the pages to come, I did my best to craft a version of those wanderings, with the hope that my own feelings of reverence might convince you that wild horses and wild places offer something big enough to make us feel humble and connected to each other—two-legged and four—all numinous, each a hallowed part of the whole.

SEARCHING FOR EQUUS

Every non-two-legged creature is a saint.

—Thomas Merton, cited in *Illuminations of Hildegard of Bingen*

Not long after Lynn and I discovered that there were wild horses in Wyoming, I began to hear legends about the bands of mustangs in the east half of the Red Desert. The myths and rumors propelled me into the arid, south-central region of the state. On dirt and gravel roads I drove in great, arching loops. I used my binoculars to scan the horizon. Small bands of horses appeared on my standard route, but in spite of my efforts, years passed without a sighting of the herds described by Bureau of Land Management (BLM) officials and mustang advocates. Even as I studied maps and took the advice that people gave me, my searches ended without any notable success. I grew suspicious. I would even say that I turned into a skeptic. It was at that time I bought a copy of *Tracking and the Art of Seeing* by Paul Rezendes. The next steps were clear, and they required more than driving around in circles with binoculars.

Last spring, I loaded a backpack in the car with the intent to hike over ridges and down into the troughs that rumple the desert.

In years past, while out driving, it often occurred to me that large groups of horses could be in the area, but hidden out of sight, behind a rise or even a bump in the landscape. With my boots on the backseat, I set out to explore.

⁘▾⣀▾⣿⣿▾⣀▾⁘

Fifteen miles north of Rawlins I leave the pavement and civilization. I look into the distance like I always do, but this time I change my approach. I begin to pay attention to the dirt. The earth offers signs of wild horses: old hoofprints, windblown and weathered. I stop to take a closer look. In *Tracking and the Art of Seeing*, Rezendes describes how the process of stalking an animal opens a window that casts light onto the shape of their lives. A good tracker reads signs the way that we read books. In fact, before the advent of paper and ink, landscapes and animal signs were the first things our ancestors made an attempt to read.

It appears that a band of three horses spent several moments walking down the side of the road. They meandered, maybe touching their shoulders together. Then one turned to look toward the south, perhaps scanning the scene for threats. The largest of the three crossed the road and then back again to rejoin the others. At the bottom of a draw they left the gravel, likely coaxed by the green grass, thriving in the shade where rain collects. I discover a row of grasses, partially eaten, but then I lose the hoofprints in the foliage.

In *Being a Beast*, Charles Foster suggests, "Animals are rolling conversations with the land from which they come and from which they exist." Still, it's a quiet conversation. Messages remain after animals make their way through a setting, but they're not the kind of messages that we usually take time to interpret. We live in cities and neighborhoods. Actually, we live inside our heads, and in our minds, we find ourselves preoccupied in a world of concepts and abstractions. When we look at a piece of undeveloped land, our brains say, "forest" or "desert" or "prairie." That is often where the conversation ends. In the poem "Description without Place," Wallace Stevens explains that we tend to live in descriptions of places as opposed to the places themselves.

We carve the world into categories. We define every piece of our habitat, and most of the time we make good use of those definitions. They help us to navigate, but the categories we create also limit our ability to detect nuance or details. They limit our ability to see. When we write off a stretch of prairie as a "grassland," for example, that makes it hard to pay attention to subtle features, the texture of the terrain. It's even harder for us to imagine the life or vision of the animals that move throughout a place.

A good tracker thinks like a beast. That raises a question, however. How do animals think? At some point, during the process of evolution, we retreated into our minds, but animals live in their bodies. We gained an awful lot as our brains spun off into words, and math, and science, and technology. But we lost something too.

Good tracking demands that you suspend the narrative unfurling in your mind and return to the raw input taken in through the senses. This project is not unique. Buddhists have been disparaging words, quieting their minds, and doing their best to live-in-the-moment for centuries. Jesuit monks do the same thing. It's typical for monks to take a vow of silence, for at least a portion of their lives. The assumption is, if you dispense with words, then it is possible to commune with the soft vibration—or the lack of noise and chatter—that we often link to the divine. Similarly, silence is often seen as the best means to commune with nature in her own language.

Quietude.

I am doing my best to try to imagine what the horses that I'm tracking saw in this ravine. I am attempting to picture how they felt. I try to guess where their attention could have been focused, but the number of horse-bitten blades of grass start to run out, and eventually I lose the direction of the band in a tangle of sage.

Back at the car, I start down the dirt road again. I find more hoofprints, but wind and rain have made the signs a challenge to read. I also see a pile of manure on the road, but it's easy to tell it has been there for a month or so. The dung is encouraging, however. The Colorado-based mustang advocate, Ginger Kathrens, coined a phrase that Lynn and I like to repeat when we're looking for horses: "Where there's poop, there's hope."

Further on, a faint and seldom-used Jeep trail intersects the road I'm driving, and at the confluence of the two paths, I find what looks like the mother of all manure piles. Three feet high and five feet wide, the horse apples stand as a testament to the strength and mystery of gastroenterology. It's an example of what we call a meta-pile. Wild horses use them as a means to communicate with others—friends and enemies alike. They build mileposts and send messages by leaving their droppings in meaningful places. This pile has existed for years. By its size, it appears that a dozen mustangs made contributions.

Our best research suggests that horses live in a world of aromas. Stallions passing by this marker dip their noses to the pile. They analyze all of the aging specimens, and if the information is compelling, horses will lift their heads and curl their upper lips to expose their teeth in what we call a flehmen response. In this posture, horses draw scented air over the vomeronasal organs in their sinuses. The equine sense of smell has been tested and discovered to be profound. From a whiff of a meta-pile, a horse can tell who left samples. They can also tell how long it's been since their friends and competitors were there. In other words: horses smell time.

When mustangs meet, they hold their faces together. That gives each animal a chance to breathe air into the nose of the other. The breath of the new acquaintance is saved and marked as an identity. Horses come to know and remember one another by the smell of the air that leaves their bodies. They experience each other, and their habitat, differently than us. When we meet someone, we lock our eyes together, briefly, and then we exchange words. We start with names and then we begin to narrate. Likewise, when human beings dream, we tend to dream in stories made up of pictures and narratives. What do horses dream? I suspect when horses go to sleep, they drift off into a vortex of aromas.

Their thoughts and memories are different from ours, but we also share some similarities. For example, mustangs love their families, and they value independence. In the era when the wild horses of the West numbered in the millions, Mexican caballeros were hired to round them up for sale as stock in the Southwest. Then, as now, the act of taking mustangs from their homes presented challenges. Horses injured themselves in the fight. In the process of being taken into custody, some died as a result of broken legs or necks. In some cases, however, the men hired to round up mustangs described stallions dying, not of physical injuries, but of broken hearts. The old cowboys called it *sentimientos*. The stallions became distraught because they missed their mares. What was it that killed them, then?

A yearning for the smell of a lover? The thought of a future where they couldn't share the same breath anymore?

I assume that the meta-pile, placed at the confluence of two dirt roads, serves as a sign. It's a message: "We came this way." A countless number of hoofprints pock the Jeep path leading to the north of the road I'm on, so I turn the car onto the two-track trail. I am easily distracted. A pair of prairie falcons circle overhead. Horned larks test their bravery by flying in front of the car, and a light breeze bounces the thin grass of the desert. After a mile of slow-motion bobbing down the trail, I see the reason for the meta-pile and the prevalence of horse tracks—a spring.

The BLM and agribusinesses maintain solar-powered water troughs in key places throughout the Red Desert. In most cases, a pump keeps a trickle of water pouring into a vessel, often a tractor tire, for most of the year. Livestock are the reason that they keep the water flowing in dry country, but horses, antelope, and herds of desert elk also partake.

This water hole is no exception. Cow pies surround the spring, along with a host of animal signs baked into the soil. In between the hoofprints of cattle, I see evidence that horses moved off further to the north after a drink. The path that I've been driving continues in the same direction, but the quality of the road changes. Sagebrush has grown tall on the hump between the tire tracks. The road also appears to have been washed out at the bottom of a draw. A Subaru Outback is a decent vehicle, but there are limits. It's a station wagon, not a monster truck.

With a pack full of food, water, and extra clothes, I start to hike. Hoofprints lead down into a gully that sees intermittent flows. I walk up and down another ridge and valley as I cut to the north across a prehistoric watershed. Then, when I make it to the top of the second rise, the terrain opens up into a wide, bowl-like valley circled by hills—and wild horses—more than I have ever seen in one setting.

I don't take time to count, but it appears that there are more than a hundred mustangs within view. A dozen bands of between six and fourteen horses graze the forage in the basin. For three years prior, I had driven in circles around the area. Mostly, I'd stuck to the BLM's official map and "scenic horse tour." I'd never seen more than a handful of animals. During that time, I questioned the government, and even other horse enthusiasts, about the presence of large numbers of mustangs in the east half of the Red Desert. As it turns out, they found a place where they could live in peace, surrounded by roads, but never seen by anybody passing through.

From the ridge, looking down onto the horses, I am struck by a familiar feeling. For most people, wild creatures hold a kind of charm. When we see an animal, the sight often yields emotion, but the sentiments differ according to the species. Bugs make us feel curious, for example. What is it like to be so small? The sight of a wolf nearly always produces a sense of respect, and sometimes fear. Bison impress us as stately. They calm us, just as long as they don't charge. Fish seem like enigmas because they live in a mysterious element. When it comes to wild horses, their beauty strikes us most, but horses possess more than prettiness. The appearance of mustangs on the landscape in the West can be beautiful, of course. But it is more. The sight and the experience cross over into the sublime. The spectacle of wild horses surrounded by scenes of rugged topography can produce a sense of reverence so strong, it feels almost unnerving.

I kneel at the top of the ridge. None of the horses have seen me yet, but I'll need to make my presence known. It's no good to try to sneak up on them. If horses find you creeping around, they assume that you harbor ill motives. When I stand up, two of the bands take notice of my silhouette. I appear out of place on terrain without any trees. Worse, I look like a predator. My two eyes are set together, right in the front of my face, just like a cat. Our bodies evolved to help us focus on the prey in front of us during a chase.

Bands of mustangs differ when it comes to what we call their "flight distance." That is, the distance they allow a threat to approach, before they flee. Some bands of wild horses run when they see a vehicle half a mile in the distance. Others will hold a hundred yards between themselves and anyone or anything that they don't know, but horses that see people regularly without incident will sometimes allow a person within fifty feet, farther than a mountain lion can jump, and enough length to give them a head start if a sprint is necessary.

In the wild, mustangs depend on their families, in particular the wisdom of their lead mares, to find food and water and to avoid danger. When I start to walk downhill toward the bottom of the basin, two bands leave immediately. One saunters away over the crest of a hill, led by their matriarch. Another makes a swift move to the other side of the valley.

When I see a band of mustangs I grab for my camera. I don't even have to think about what to do. I don't know if I would call it an instinct, but I feel a strong impulse. As a species, human beings are attuned to aesthetics. When we see something that pleases our eye, the first thing we do is: we stare. We use our vision to collect an image of what lies before us, so we can store a likeness in our minds. Once we've made a mental archive of a sight we like, then it is ours to recall, over and over. Beauty demands replication.

When we are young, teachers and parents give us art supplies. We're taught to ogle things we like and reproduce them on paper. Later on, in adolescence, our culture conspires to convince us that we are "not creative," so we abandon our sketchbooks. But there are few occasions where technology is not appropriate in our society, so we carry cameras, now more than ever.

The engineers who designed cell phones did not have to scratch their heads too long to figure out what it would take to make a phone hard to put down—visual images. The companies that manufacture phones did not create our obsession with applications like Facebook and Instagram, however. They just exploited one of our weaknesses. We're vulnerable to the people, places, and animals that we find beautiful. In "The Arrow," the poet William Butler Yeats wrote this of someone that he found appealing: "I thought of your beauty / and this arrow / made out of a wild thought / is in my marrow." Beauty seizes our attention and lodges itself in our thinking. Further still, beauty compels. The genealogy of the word "beauty" includes a relation to the Greek term *kalien*, which contains the notion of a summon or beckoning.

Down the hill I go, slowly, making my way toward the horses nearest to me. It's a family of four mustangs: a stallion, two mares, and a yearling. All of them watch, and my presence gives them a reason to stop eating, but they're not bothered enough to leave. As

I approach, the stallion moves to the front of the group to serve as guard, and that is my signal. I stop where I am, and while I'm still I take a knee.

When male horses become band stallions, they undergo a transformation. Their bodies release testosterone to correspond with their responsibilities. The chests and hindquarters of stallions grow heavy with muscle, their faces develop a chiseled appearance, and their jowls become prominent. I make a subtle move to the left, and then the right. I am trying to capture the family in a single image, but the stallion won't let me have a view of the whole band. He keeps himself between me and them, so I decide to just sit down. It's a nice day. I have three liters of water and plenty of food. I can wait.

After ten minutes, the horses start to relax. They go back to eating and I join them by chewing on a granola bar. Eventually, the stallion drifts off to the side, away from the mares, but they're all focused on the grass in front of them. They're not looking up to pose for photographs. After twenty minutes, the yearling walks over to her father. When she reaches him, he lifts his head. He gives her a nuzzle to acknowledge her presence. With a nod, he rubs his cheek on hers to let her know that everything is fine, even in spite of the human tucked in the grass, crunching on a granola bar. *Click. Click.* My shutter clacks.

The horses hear the motorbike before I can. It's faint. The stallion I am watching turns his ears toward the west, and the lead mare in the band starts to head for the opposite side of the basin. The family follows her. Then after a moment, they are gone. The other bands in the valley watch them move, and it starts to make them uneasy. By this point, I hear the buzz of the dirt bike and all of the horses hear it too. Some of the bands act sooner than others, but after three minutes' worth of commotion I find myself alone.

I gather my things and hike up toward the ridge that's hiding the horses. It is easy to locate the hoofprints that they made as they fled from the sound of the motorcycle. At the top of the hill, I expect to find them in the next valley over. Instead, I find four more empty ridgelines stretching toward the east. It took me a while to even reach the summit that I'm standing on, and I am a long way from the car, so I decide to end the search.

Back in the bottom of the basin, I take a moment to look around and remember the largest group of wild horses I had ever seen. While I'm walking, I notice a high point on the opposite side of the valley. It looks like it might offer a scenic view to the west.

It's getting late, but not too late. On the climb up, I find signs that horses have been there: hoofprints and partially eaten tufts of grass. I follow the tracks to the top, where my suspicion is confirmed. The high mark on the hill offers a vantage point. The sun fills the valley below with late-afternoon light. I don't see any horses from where I stand, but I see tracks leading downward. I follow them as far as I can with my eyes, and it appears that they lead to a set of rock formations a third of the way down the slope, on a terrace with an overlook.

I follow the hoofprints to a spot where boulders the size of minivans jut up through sage and cactus. For a stretch of fifty yards, at least somewhat in a circle, rows of rocks stand up like pillars. It feels like I am looking at the top of an old fortress, buried eons ago under a sea of soil.

Among the rocks I find evidence that it's a place where groups of mustangs spend their time. I find three meta-piles of dung in the vicinity. Traces of hair cling to a crack in a rock at shoulder height—a station where they rub their necks. Hoofprints whorl in circles as bands of mustangs once arranged themselves for grooming or to swat flies with their tails. Sharp changes in the direction of the prints mark a skirmish. I also find a plateau in between rocks where horses rolled over onto their backs. It's one of their favorite activities. When they feel happy and unthreatened, mustangs will find a spot where they can roll back and forth with their legs in the air, covering themselves in dust. This is one such place. The signs suggest that wild horses find meaning in these ramparts of stone.

Fifty miles to the west, anthropologists discovered a trove of petroglyphs on a similar rock formation. Native people were drawn to the sharp relief in a landscape that tends toward more incremental folds. Native people found significance in the sandstone walls, so much that they took time to add art to the vertical surfaces, pictures with cultural and historic value, images that say to others: "We were here."

It starts to feel like I am standing in the middle of something that amounts to a wild horse version of Easter Island or Stonehenge. Or maybe it's a church. In any case—a location of substance. It's a site that mustangs hold in their memories, somewhere that they return to, a place where they roll and fight and mate and scratch their necks and groom each other. Horses do not paint or sculpt. They're not as visual as us. Because they live in a world of aromas, when they want to mark a location as meaningful, they leave coordinated mounds of manure. The piles contain a message: "We were here."

Now they are gone. I sit at the base of a rock and wait. The site affords me a long view of the Red Desert. The shadows of evening reveal soft rows of silhouettes on a landscape that can appear stark and menacing in the middle of the day. In *Desert Solitaire* Edward Abbey wrote, with respect to our dry regions, "The desert lies there like the bare skeleton of being … inviting not love but contemplation."

Abbey was right about deserts. You have to be careful, though. My experience has been, in the dry parts of our world, we walk a fine line between the reverie of solitude and something that can become ominous. Like wild horses themselves, the places where they live are more than just beautiful, they are sublime, and sublimity comes with a hazardous edge. Deserts are pleasing to most of our eyes, but they are more. They are foreboding. With small amounts of water, they protect privileged forms of life, but they also surround you with a geography of thirst, an unceasing reminder of your own mortality.

It's a fully formed and wholly uneaten bunch of blue grama grass that pulls me out of my ruminations. I attempt to decide if it is blue or green and I determine it is both. Right here in the middle of the Red Desert, this spiky tuft is blue and green. The unlikely plant makes me think about a passage from the work of Joseph Wood Krutch. In an article called "The Miracle of Grass," he wrote:

Of all the green things that make up what Goethe called 'the living garment of God,' grass is the humblest, the most nearly omnipresent, and the most stupidly taken for granted ... a miracle so common that we no longer regard it as miraculous.

The evening sun casts a revealing light on the blades of grass in front of me, so I crouch down and make an image, and then another. The scene strikes me as picturesque. Not just the plant necessarily, but the moment.

Time has an aesthetic. I linger for a second because it feels like the sort of juncture where you find yourself staring at a bundle of cut flowers or out the window at the last snowfall of winter—there, but in a sense already gone. I continue to follow hoofprints on my way back to the water hole: evidence of horses, still enchanting, even after they've set off for something else.

SOULS OF WILDNESS

We need another and a wiser and perhaps a more mystical concept of animals.

—Henry Beston, *The Outermost House*

A s a kid, I rode a pony with a painted coat. My family called her "Daisy." She could run faster than any of the horses within five miles of our house. She beat thoroughbreds. Arabians. Once, she outran a quarter horse. I loved that pony. I loved her right up until the point when I discovered motocross. After that, my attention to horses waned. I developed a crush on metal and plastic. I still live in a world of machines and technology, but a mountain bike replaced the motorcycle. Pedals are quieter than pistons. Even so, after leaving home, I went two decades without horses in my life. In retrospect, it feels like I found them again, or they found me, at the right time.

As a young person, I was not prepared to think about the significance of horses. I considered them excellent pets, and maybe even friends, but I was not ready to think about their evolution, their role in our culture, or the place they hold in human history. By midlife,

I suppose most of us start to drift in the direction of big, persistent questions like "What does it all mean?" For my part, the discovery that wild horses still roam the West gave me a chance to entertain some of the questions that afflict people of a certain age. At the same time, my first encounter with mustangs also left me with something close to a childlike feeling of fascination.

On the day when Lynn and I found out that there were wild horses living in the West, we had not set out to make any such discovery. We had actually planned a fishing trip to the Hole-in-the-Wall area of Wyoming. It's a landscape of red cliffs and mesas. Butch Cassidy and the Sundance Kid used to hide in the vicinity, among the bluffs along the Middle Fork of the Powder River. I was looking forward to a weekend of fly fishing for trout, but the universe had something different in mind. Before we even made it to the stream, our course had changed. We stumbled onto a band of mustangs, and I felt a sense of curiosity that's kept me searching ever since.

On the highway west of Casper, we run into rain. Then the rain turns into a full-throated storm, and we find ourselves pressing into wind-driven hail. I see a patch of blue sky on my left, so I ask, "Would you like to see the Red Desert?" I met Lynn in Tucson. She likes deserts. She says, "Sure. Go left. Look. There's a road." It doesn't take long to escape the weather. Soon, we're heading south with the sun beating through the windshield. As the dirt and vegetation dry, I begin to see horses. I assume that we're on public land. I ask, "Whose horses?" Then I point out that we are probably on public property. Lynn says, "I don't know." Then she looks at a map.

After a moment, she says, "We're on a herd area run by the Bureau of Land Management. Those are wild horses."

Wild horses. Wild? Wild is one of my favorite adjectives. I didn't know Lynn when she was young, but she grew up with horses too. "Why don't we stop?" she asks.

I dig my camera out of the backseat. Then I unfold a tripod, clean the surface of my most powerful lens, and we start to trek through the sagebrush. When we saw the horses from the car, they were grazing. But when we start hiking, they begin to show signs of alertness. They don't stop eating, but they lift their heads to check our location. We push onward, closer to them. We shorten the distance until thirty yards stand between us. After that, they start to walk.

Through my telephoto lens, I see their coats. Scrapes and scars mark the terrain between their shoulders and haunches. Manes jut in between their ears to cover up their eyes. One forehead sports a cluster of burrs. They form a gnarled hat of hair and dehydrated plants. In another instance, a dreadlock hangs from one of their necks. These are nobody's horses. They are scrappy. They're unkempt—and they are magnificent.

In 1868, a man by the name of Peres stumbled onto the mouth of a cavern in the hills of northern Spain. He described the spot to an archeologist, Marcelino Sautuola. Years later, Sautuola ventured to the cave with his daughter and a pair of oil lamps. Once they were inside, she noticed familiar shapes on the ceiling and walls, "Look. Animals." They discovered the Altamira site. The cave hosts one of the oldest and most elaborate collections of rock art ever found.

The images include examples of deer and bison, but the stars of the exhibit are horses. Altamira represents an early effort to capture the majesty of the world with a two-dimensional image: one of our first attempts at art. When human groups began to explore aesthetics, they did their best to mirror the form and essence of the horse.

As human beings, we're inconsistent when it comes to our tastes. At one time, we preferred our automobiles with exaggerated fins jutting up toward the back. Today, we like sleek cars. Bell-bottomed pants sometimes come into vogue, and then they turn into symbols of heedless style. In our past, women used to wear the bodies of flamingos on their heads. I'm glad to say, today, we consider that kind of fashion excessive. Desires change. Still, I have searched, and I cannot find a time when we did not see dignity and seemliness in horses.

Lynn and I spend the morning trying to move in closer to the herd. I'm hoping to make a photo of their faces. We know better than to march up to them, however. We move ten feet toward them every few minutes. We talk in soft tones, so they know that we are not two-legged cats trying to stalk up on them in silence. We do not walk in straight lines. We tack left and right to convince them that we're just two friendly bipeds out meandering on the prairie, but it doesn't work. Each time we step closer, the horses look up from the ground. They spot us. Then they readjust their position. After a long pursuit in slow motion, we are half a mile from our car. I'm starting to get hungry, and it's been too long since we drank any water. We decide to head back to the road. I untie the flannel shirt that I've been wearing on my waist, but before I put my arms into the sleeves, I flap it to shake off the dust. I flick it down and then back up. When I do that, it makes a loud *crack* of a sound.

Stampede.

One moment the horses are grazing and the next they're flying through the sage. No transition. When the sound of my shirt reaches their ears, the landscape shifts. The calm swells of the prairie roil into a storm of motion. The horses run away from us in the beginning. Then a band of four breaks to the right. They make a wide turn. We watch as they bend their route. They circle around until it appears that they are running back toward us.

Then it becomes clear that they *are* running toward us. I hear Lynn say, "Oh." It's not a word, however. It's more like a sound. I'm speechless too. I grab my wife and pull her beside me. We stand together behind the camera, which is mounted on top of a tripod. It's not a bunker, but it's all we have.

We've spent long parts of our lives in places where risks hide, barely out of view. We are educated when it comes to safety in the wilderness. We know what to do if we're attacked by a black bear, or a grizzly, or a mountain lion. We've taken time to practice, so we can act without having to think about the best course in case of emergency. None of our training prepared us to protect ourselves from a stampede of wild horses, so we stand together, making sounds from behind an aluminum tripod. It is sad, but in a way, a little romantic.

We can't take our eyes off of the mustangs. Their legs churn the dry grasses. They kick up a squall of dust. Then they come to a halt. Ten feet away, the hooves of the lead horse dig in the dirt and they all stop. Dust clouds our view, but when it clears, the horses emerge: chests heaving, nostrils flared, and ears in fighting position.

The two of us turn into sculptures of ourselves. At first, I look ahead, but even blinking feels like an act of aggression. I turn my eyes toward the ground. Then I realize that I am no longer breathing, so I remind myself to inhale. I hear Lynn trying to keep herself from crying. We stay this way for what feels like five minutes. Maybe more. We're stuck in a standoff, with fear and curiosity as glue, binding us to the horses.

I whisper, "I'm going to make a picture."

Lynn says, "Yeah. Slowly. Don't make any noises."

The camera utters a beep as it brings the lens into focus. The sound attracts the horses' attention. Their ears lock onto the black box at the top of the tripod. They look bothered, but then after a moment, they start to relax. The quiet clicks and chirps actually seem to put them at ease. I suspect the sounds make us seem safe—a pair of birds, more like chubby cranes than grizzlies.

After I've made enough pictures, I look up from my view-finder. I stand for several minutes, staring eye to eye at the "other." The Sioux and the Cheyenne called them "The Horse People." This band's leader is a male that we've seen often in the time since our first encounter. We guess that he's an old stallion, spending his golden years roaming with a group of bachelors. His body is charcoal. A dark coat covers his back and shoulders, but it breaks up along his neck. Under his throat, the color changes to a marbled spread of black and white. On his face, he wears a set of marks that give him a luminous appearance. As I look into his eyes, I am struck by the sense that I'm looking through history. It feels like I am looking into the eye of the earth.

Horses evolved here on the North American continent. They evolved here and nowhere else. They grazed alongside woolly mammoths. They ran from the threat of dire wolves and saber-toothed cats. Paleontologists suggest that horses went extinct in this hemisphere during the last ice age. At least, that's one story. The fossil record demonstrates that horses outlasted other species in the Pleistocene, and some evidence suggests that small bands may have survived into the era of European conquest. Even so, we can assume at some point most or all of them migrated over the Bering land bridge into what is now Siberia.

From the steppes of Eurasia, the animals traveled to Africa and across Europe. Some of them eventually took on stripes and evolved into zebras. The Botai people of Kazakhstan were the first to climb onto horses' backs. Then the herdsmen of the Mediterranean used them to launch war parties into Spain. Not to be outdone, the Spaniards also began to keep horses. Riding became an art. Finally, in the days of Christopher Columbus, horses were loaded on ships and returned to the homeland of their ancestors. The native people of the West have a saying, "The grass remembers the horses." The tribes of the plains found spiritual partners in these animals, whose teeth and hooves evolved on American soil.

In spite of their role on farms and in militaries, anyone who has witnessed a band of wild mustangs running can see that their bodies were carved by the elements of western states: prairie wind and wide-open spaces. Compared to the other animals that we turned into pets or commodities, horses wear their domestication lightly. After a single generation is born in freedom, they return to the patterns of behavior that served them since the Cenozoic. Like the offspring of hatchery-raised salmon born into rivers, they only know one state—the wild.

In his essay called "Walking," first published in the *Atlantic* in 1862, Henry David Thoreau suggested, "In wildness is the preservation of the world." It is one of the most enigmatic sentences in American letters. Speculations about what he meant abound in different directions, but most scholars agree that the hermit of Walden used these words to remind us that societies can take a toll on our better nature. In towns and cities, our culture goes to work on us. *We* become domesticated. Our thoughts turn into reflections of popular, but often dubious beliefs.

Our culture limits our vision. Societies ask us to wear a set of blinders, much like those that we would place onto the eyes of a draft horse. Blinders curb what you see. They make it possible for us to look at human beings as if they are one-dimensional. For instance, we tend to see each other, and even ourselves, as simple workers or mere consumers. When we look at the dry grasses of our prairies and deserts, too often, we dwindle what we see to that of a forage factory, a pasture for sheep and cattle, or an economic entity, thought of in terms of animal-units-per-month. Thoreau would not have pictured the prairie that way. He saw a rich palette of both humanity and nature, stretching from his feet toward the West.

At times, we rise above the tendency to shrink our thoughts on land, people, and animals down to the level of simple utilitarianism. For example, in 1971, Richard Nixon signed the Wild and

Free-Roaming Horses and Burros Act. When we crafted the legislation that protects wild horses, we stood up for aesthetic values and the moral case for conserving their habitat. In contrast, today, I often hear the American mustang discussed as a "nuisance." People describe them as out of place. They call them pests and misfits.

I do not take issue with the notion that wild horses are misfits. They belong to another era—a time when the grasslands of this continent were still untamed. For that reason alone, we ought to appreciate mustangs. During a speech on civil rights, the Reverend Martin Luther King joined with Thoreau by placing faith in wildness. King said, "Human salvation lies in the hands of the creatively maladjusted." Misfits. Those who don't wear blinders. People who refuse to follow.

On some level, we understand what the wisest among us have tried to teach. In some ways, we acknowledge the value of wildness. We admire those with a will strong enough to overcome the pressure to conform. The mustang serves as a mascot for one of the high schools in our hometown: Casper, Wyoming. Since we lack a professional football team, most of us cheer for the Denver Broncos, and every vehicle registered in the state bears a license plate emblazoned with an image of a bucking horse. In some sense, we know the value and appeal of a rebel. We identify with the spirit of the mustang. We made the wild horse into a symbol of unbrokenness.

We also decreased the number of mustangs in the West from as many as 5 million to less than 80,000 in two generations. The state of Wyoming recently sued the Bureau of Land Management. If the state wins the lawsuit, the ruling will force the BLM to further reduce the number of wild horses within our borders. In addition, state representatives routinely pitch proposals to lift our current ban on horse slaughter. John Fire Lame Deer, a member of the Lakota Sioux tribe, once told an interviewer, "When a people start killing off their own symbols, they are in a bad way."

After an hour, the horses in front of us turn their attention to one another. They start to nuzzle each other's faces and necks. One of them looks like he is sleeping. I fold the tripod and we begin to make our way toward the car. We haven't even taken time to pick a place to camp. Our original plans would have put us on a creek a hundred miles to the north. After we walk several paces, I cannot help myself. I turn around. The horses have begun to follow us. They do not walk us all the way back to the road, but they follow for fifty yards, and then they watch us leave.

Back home, Monday morning, I throw a leg over my mountain bike and start the usual commute to work. I begin on a well-worn path: two lefts and then a right on the paved grid of our neighborhood. Before I reach the office, I notice I am running early, so I jump the curb. Then I take off into the empty grassland at the edge of town.

I'VE COME TO LOOK FOR AMERICA

Mankind will not perish for want of information, but only for want of appreciation.

—Abraham Joshua Heschel, *God in Search of Man*

It is important that we find animals to love.

—Thomas McGuane, *Some Horses*

I've been missing get-togethers. The day after a neighborhood poker game, I learned that my friend Jim had asked about my absence, "Where is Hanson?" In response, my colleague Brad sang a line from a song by Jonathon Richman: "*I ain't seen him much / since he / started with horses.*" It is true. In the past several years, I've spent my spare time on the prairies of Wyoming with a camera pointed at bands of mustangs. Sometimes I go by myself. Other times I travel with Lynn. Either way, if there's a blank spot on the calendar, I don't have to think about how to fill the days. I load the car and drive to places where I'm likely to find horses.

Wild mustangs are not my first obsession. Two decades' worth of out-of-control fly fishing for trout revealed the first. At one point,

I also thought I would retrace the canoe routes of the French fur traders and explorers. I paddled a lot of water before I gave up on that ghost. I became a bird-watcher. In my thirties, I invested in a pair of binoculars and a bookshelf full of field guides. Over time, my home became a warehouse for equipment that I take with me when I leave home. That's typical. American lives, more so than most, unfold in the form of arrivals and departures. We wander to a degree that can feel nomadic.

In the middle 1900s, we left the era of agriculture. By the end of the last century, few of us lived on farms or ranches. The production of food became an industrial process, alongside manufacturing. In the past, we put more into our land when we wanted to get ahead. Today, we move to find new opportunities. Our careers keep us in motion. Then—when we are free from our responsibilities—we go. We take a vacation.

Some of us leave in order to escape. I know families that take annual trips to Walt Disney World in Florida. I can't think of a better way to take flight from contemporary life. The attraction is the absence of reality. Critics charge the Walt Disney Company and its customers with living in denial. They accuse Disney of providing a distraction from the injustices that unfold inside our nation, but the Disney critics miss the point. The purpose of a trip to Disney World is to take a break from wrongdoings and injustice. It's the "Magic Kingdom." It is not the "Kingdom Where We Give Thought to the Sober-and-Frequently-Sad Reality of Life in a Twenty-First Century Society." Vacations built around distractions often serve us well. Who among us doesn't need a break sometimes?

The culture that we live in often makes us feel like escaping, but we travel for reasons other than to flee. Americans are seekers too. We search when we travel. Many of us put ourselves in motion as a way to make a "pilgrimage," whether we use that word to describe our journeys. As opposed to tourism as a diversion from the day to day, the pilgrimage offers a way to add a meaningful element to what, eventually, becomes a life story.

We set the largest share of our chapters at home. We connect our identities to the places where we live, but travel-as-search allows us to expand the edges of the self. Away from families and jobs, we forget the memories we don't want to recall. Then we replace them by adding paragraphs, or even whole new chapters, to our stories. We don't come all the way back from a pilgrimage. We return different. When we set out to explore, we gain something. We lose things too.

Wild horses go where they want. They roam over deserts, through forests, and on top of mountains. You can find them in all of these places, but they favor prairies. Horses browse. That means that they can eat a range of plants, but they prefer grasses. When I watch them, sometimes I wonder what it would feel like to walk on a landscape that is edible. When they are hungry, horses lower their necks and bite off a piece of food. But horses are also prey. Foals and yearlings fall victim to cougars. That's another reason they prefer the wide open. Horses can run. Open space gives them room to dash away if they are chased. On grasslands, their bellies are full, and they are free.

Horses gravitate to prairies. It took me years to appreciate the plains, however. Like most of us in the United States, I had been socialized to see beauty in high country—pine forests, snow-covered slopes, and jagged peaks. We're taught that landscapes are worthy of our attention when they are tilted up toward the sky. For example, you can cross 300 miles of Wyoming plains without driving by a single designated "scenic" point. When you reach the Tetons, however, you find roadside parking lots every two miles, spread along the whole base of the range. The lots are full of cars and the sound of shutters clacking behind the lenses of cameras. Willa Cather is rumored to have said, "Anyone can love the mountains, but it takes soul to love the prairie."

It took a while before I started to see grasslands as a destination as opposed to someplace to race through on my way to mountainsides. The change involved a re-education. In reading about the river routes of fur trappers, I happened on an account of a conversation between a French explorer and a member of the Cree Nation from the northern part of Saskatchewan. The two had just met, so the trapper took time to explain where he had been. He described the forests and ridges of the Canadian Rockies. He did so with enthusiasm. Imagining the landscape that the trapper had described, the Cree man asked, "Is it as beautiful as the land-with-no-sticks?" The line forced me to wonder. No trees? No sticks? Beautiful? On her first visit to Wyoming, a friend from Minnesota mentioned in a somber tone, "It's treeless." I replied, "No. It's *tree-free*. Look. You can see for miles. There is nothing in your way."

We spend our lives negotiating social boundaries. For example, we live in communities made out of rules: don't turn left until you see the green arrow, don't wear flip-flop sandals to work, don't let your boss know what you really think. We build identities that bind our potential: "I'm a nurse, I don't have time for poetry," or "I'm a salesperson, I'm not a scientist." We also carve our world into compartments: this is a bedroom, living room, office, store, park, restaurant.

On large swaths of the prairie, there are no such distinctions. No lines to cross. It's all periphery: you, grass, and the horizon. In the context of our limited lives, we're only offered a handful of glimpses into boundlessness: the sea, the stars, and the prairie. In one of the lessons passed down by students of the Buddha, a long-suffering man was said to have asked him, "What is paradise?" The Buddha replied, "Emptiness."

I grew up in the 1970s watching the TV show *Grizzly Adams*. Once a week for an hour I sat down to watch "Adams" make his way in the West of the 1800s. In his hometown, he was accused of a crime that he did not commit, so to avoid an unjust punishment, Adams ran to the mountains. He lived in a log cabin. He befriended miners, Native Americans, and animals. Adams shared his life with one animal in particular, a grizzly bear named "Ben." He rescued the bruin from a perilous fate on the side of a cliff when he was just a cub. From then on, Adams and the grizzly were inseparable. Stories about the relationship between a man and an animal offered viewers a contrast to the urban sprawl growing in circles around them.

Some decades are reflective. In the 1960s and 1970s, many of us started to assess the future offered to us in our culture. We started questioning what we call the "establishment." Americans were reading books like *The Lonely Crowd* and *The Man in the Grey Flannel Suit*. As a group, we started to wonder if we wanted what the United States economy had to offer—namely, lives tethered to either a desk or an assembly line. At the time, when we looked at our collective self in the mirror, we saw single-minded, corporate types. When we looked at our surroundings, we saw the ruin caused by those same single-minded corporate types. News reports described litter, smog, and pollution. The songwriter Neil Young captured the spirit of the day with a lyric that implored us to *"look at Mother Nature / on the run / in the 1970s."* The words resonated. Real estate developers were gobbling up land. We were driving animals to extinction. The surface of a river in Ohio caught on fire.

During the 1980s, lust for profit reclaimed its status in the United States, but in the two decades prior, we questioned the corporate agenda—for ourselves and for the world. In contrast to business suits, people aspired to wear cut-off blue jeans and t-shirts. An entire generation became interested in getting "back to nature." Many saw the outdoors as a kind of haven where people could take refuge from self-interest and competition. Grizzly Adams appealed to viewers. He didn't compete. He cooperated with everyone. He didn't drive anything to extinction. He treated animals with kindness. Creatures walked up to him without fear. It's an old story, one that predates the 1970s. For as long as human beings have been the dominant predators on the planet, we have dreamed of a scenario where we could commune, peacefully, with other species. It is biblical. The lion lies down with the lamb.

Horses evolved as prey. The height and weight of the 55-million-year-old "dawn pony" matched that of a medium-sized dog. Over the ages, the animals became larger, faster, and more powerful. At each step, horses grew more capable of protecting each other.

The eyes of the horse became the largest of the land mammals. They can see on both sides of their bodies. The only blind spots they possess lie right in front of them and back behind their tails. Apart from those two places, their field of vision includes 340 degrees of longitude. Horses also developed the ability to remember. Their recollections last for years. From an evolutionary standpoint, the capacity to store memories has served horses. If they are threatened in a specific place or by a particular type of animal, they don't forget.

When Lynn and I started making photographs of mustangs, the horses usually appeared as small, colored dots on the landscape. Most of the stallions would not allow us close to their bands. Over the course of a year, however, two of the families near our home grew to accept our presence. We're careful to wear the same kind of clothes each time we hike out to find them. For example, I wear a wide-brimmed hat. I even wear it on cloudy days. I want the horses to see me and remember, "That's the guy with the hat. He's alright. He never tries to attack anyone." Over time, the plan started to work. Bands that used to run or walk away now allow us to approach within a hundred feet or less.

Horses are bigger than we are. Standing alongside a wild animal that can weigh in excess of a thousand pounds feels profound. When I spend time in their company, I am often overwhelmed by a sense that I stand at a crossroads where the legends of the West meet the blood and bone. Reality. I've spent my adult life searching, in a variety of places and by a range of means, for the mythical West. I have fished high country lakes for cutthroat trout. I've paddled whitewater rivers. I have climbed to the tops of mountains and I've descended into canyons too.

It turns out the West of my imagination is the one with a mustang in the foreground.

Even though I grew up with horses, that did not prepare me for the creatures I've seen on our public lands. There is a difference between domestic animals and those born free. Domestic horses live in a constant state of having their nature bent and tempered by a master. In contrast, horses born into the wild possess the same tendencies that the species developed over the course of its evolution. One such tendency involves the establishment of a hierarchy, with regard to the dominant males and females in a family. Wild horses bite and kick, and they collide. In the process, they determine leadership roles and breeding rights. Another of their behaviors includes watching for danger. Horses have been known to increase the size of their herds, to the point where numerous bands come together, in areas where they face threats from mountain lions.

It is this orientation—toward the welfare of the whole—that affects me the most. As herbivores, mustangs do not have fangs. They do not possess claws. All they have going for them in a fight is size, their speed, and each other. It is not an accident that they form bands. They draw strength and comfort from their place within a group. During the spring, wild horses battle to establish levels of dominance, but when the roughhousing is over, and families have taken shape, they turn toward their relationships with each other.

I've been astounded by the bonds of affection that bind horses. They put their long, artfully chiseled faces next to each other. They nuzzle with their noses and lips. They use their teeth to scratch each other's backs. They know the spots that are hard to reach on an equine body—withers and shoulder blades, for example—so they help each other by nibbling in all the right places. Siblings and parents stand side by side. Then they swat flies from one another's faces with their tails. Bands of mustangs spend entire afternoons preening and caring for their families.

There are few sounds. Horses whinny if they need the attention of the others. They blow out through their noses as a way to sigh and maintain contact, especially in cases where foraging carries them afield. A stallion will sometimes shriek in the presence of a rival. Apart from these examples, and the sound of the wind in the grass, mustangs live in a quiet world. As prey to carnivores, it behooves horses to maintain stealth. From an evolutionary standpoint, silence suits them. It's adaptive.

Horses fasten themselves to one another. They use their physical presence and their eyes to choreograph their position and movements. We are accustomed to seeing flocks of birds flying in unison. We are familiar with the idea that groups of fish form schools and coordinate their movements through currents and tides, but on this continent, we see few cases of large mammals sprinting together. When you see a band of wild horses run, the image tends to last. The oldest or most dominant female, the lead mare, usually begins a charge. Other members of the family step into formation. Then the stallion falls in behind them. Legs start to roll. The group floats over the prairie like they were wrought from one body of metaphysical horseness.

Mustangs are other-centered. Out of necessity, they focus their attention outward, into the workings of the band. We're social too, but not like horses. Our capacity to manipulate words gives us an inner life. We live inside a bubble made of memories.

Horses use their minds to recall threats or places of danger. We have little to fear, so we use our brains to craft personal narratives. No matter where you go or who you spend time with, you can find human beings telling and then retelling the story of themselves. We're so vigilant about maintaining our stories that we become preoccupied. We think about ourselves to the exclusion of others. Our evolution was atypical. We've turned into the rarest of creatures: self-centered, but at the same time, bound to live in groups.

Standing on the prairie with the last remaining wild horses on the continent is riveting. The animals capture your attention. It takes all of your senses to absorb the setting: splendor, peace, and motion. You strain your eyes. Your heart beats, notably, inside your chest. You have to remind yourself to exhale. Such moments arrest your concentration. They lock you in the present. The past, the future, hopes and recollections—gone. In such an instance, when all of your memories vanish, you disappear too. You can try to hang on to the narratives inside your head. I've tried that once or twice, but I find it's better to give in to the spell. I use my time on the prairie as a way to forget myself. Oddly, it's the occasions meaningful enough to force us to forget ourselves that grow to become the standout chapters in our stories.

I spend summers, and a good part of the other seasons, standing on the plains in the company of wild horses. In the time I pass on the grasslands, there are other tasks to which I should devote attention, but my obligations have to wait. Still, there are people with whom I ought to spend more of my time. I regret the trade-offs. It is true that my friends have not seen much of me since I started with horses. As a consolation, however, I also see quite a bit less of me.

We earn our vacations. It's useful to treat entertainment as a way to sidestep roles and commitments. Movie theaters and restaurants serve a purpose, so do theme parks. Magic Kingdoms like Disneyland and Disney World offer guests a valuable way to try on new selves: yellow sarongs, Bermuda shorts, beach hats, and sunglasses. A pilgrimage provides us with something different, however. Meaningful journeys send us on a search, and while we seek, we set ourselves aside. The act of searching holds the potential to elevate the object of the quest up to the level of the sacred: shrinking egos, granting humility, and sending us back to the world with a story built upon the fulfilment of a purpose.

DAKOTA WINTER

Nature and animals frequently call us to our truest selves, call us to a response. And response is the root of the word *responsibility*.

—Charles Bergman, *Every Penguin in the World*

Last winter, Lynn and I scheduled a trip to the Black Hills Wild Horse Sanctuary in South Dakota. We'd been there before. This time we'd been camping in the forest outside of Spearfish. Before heading back to Wyoming, we looked at a map, and the name of a town caught our attention: "Hot Springs." Those two words appealed to us.

The author Dayton Hyde established the sanctuary for rescued mustangs on the shore of the Cheyenne River. The property includes 11,000 acres' worth of valley. The waters of the Cheyenne nourish a meadow on one side, and a row of cliffs guard the other. When he was alive, Hyde maintained a ranch house for himself and a bunkhouse for guests, along with a barn and a series of outbuildings. Early in the effort, Hyde also created the Institute of Range and the American Mustang (IRAM), a nonprofit operating on the grounds.

When Lynn and I made our first visit to the sanctuary, we agreed that the valley seemed like a refuge for more than just horses. It felt like a sanctuary for people frazzled by our culture. When you drive into the Cheyenne River bottom, you enter a region with marginal internet and cell service. Turkeys cross the road in front of you at an unhurried pace, and when you make it to Hyde's ranch, you find yourself greeted by wild horses squinting in the sun.

Hyde felt moved to create a sanctuary for mustangs after he'd been to a holding pen for free-roaming horses. The animals had been taken off of public property by the Bureau of Land Management. The sight of the once proud creatures standing side by side, up to their ankles in their own feces, insulted his sense of ethics. From the time he was thirteen, Hyde had worked on cattle ranches. He grew accustomed to roundups and feed lots, but the mustang holding pen struck him as wrong.

Hyde's values match those of our wisdom traditions. The Hindu concept of *ahimsa*, for example, suggests that we bear the weight of a moral obligation to refrain from harming other creatures. Along the same line, in his *Selected Writings*, the German theologian and Dominican pastor Meister Eckhart made the claim that "every single creature is full of God and a book about God," worthy of a type of respect that rises to the level of devotion.

Hyde came of age in the company of the wild horses that wander the Oregon deserts. He compared his memories of mustangs with the animals that he saw in captivity. The horses held by the BLM had formerly possessed the vigor and strength needed to survive on the prairie, but the animals before him in the pen looked deflated. In one interview, Hyde described a stallion looking at him with "sad eyes." The moment forced him to rethink his life. In the eyes of the imprisoned horse, Hyde stood there representing a set of morals gone awry. He decided to redirect his future—from ranching to building a sanctuary for mustangs.

Two generations before, in 1950, a similar event affected Velma Bronn Johnston. On her morning drive to work in Reno, Nevada, she found herself in traffic, behind a semi-tractor carrying what looked like too many horses. Blood dripped from the floor of the trailer. She followed the truck until it turned into the loading dock of a slaughterhouse. At the time, groups of rustlers held roundups of wild horses. They chased them with Jeeps and planes. Then they sold the mustangs to meat packers who ground them into canned dog food. The sight of bloody horses, and the knowledge of their fate, inspired Johnston to become a lobbyist. She became known as "Wild Horse Annie." Her efforts, and those of many others, led to the passage of the Wild and Free-Roaming Horses and Burros Act.

Something transformative accompanies the sight of horses in distress. In 1889, the German philosopher Nietzsche fell victim to a mental collapse after watching a coach driver whipping a horse in Turin, Italy. According to observers, Nietzsche ran to the animal and threw his arms around its neck. He used his body to shield the horse from any further suffering. Then he refused to let her go. Onlookers eventually convinced a policeman to intervene. The incident marked the beginning of what became a long journey into madness.

Nietzsche spent his productive years penning novels that exalted the power of the individual. In his book *God Is Dead*, he urged

Christians to ignore the value they place on compassion. Instead, he encouraged readers to admire "supermen" with traits that placed them over those that he described as "weaklings." Until the time of the incident in Turin, Nietzsche used his publications, and a faculty position at the University of Basel, to disseminate his views. He implored people to use their strengths to meet their goals at the expense of others. When discussing the relationships between and among us, Nietzsche favored the exercise of power—an arrangement where the strong rule the vulnerable. He clung to his beliefs until the day he watched a man beating a horse.

I think it's their innocence. They're herbivores. They have needs, of course: food, water, and family. Stallions tussle with each other in order to win the affection of mares, but otherwise they don't hurt anyone. Horses possess no hidden motives or agendas. They're ingenuous, and they are beautiful. Art historians describe Leonardo da Vinci's unfinished sculpture of an Iberian stallion as his greatest work—even more highly regarded than his other works—the *Mona Lisa* and *The Last Supper*, for example.

As an artist, architect, and man of science, da Vinci considered the mathematics of beauty. The angles, proportion, and symmetry of the equine body provided him with the consummate subject. Leonardo crafted the prototype of the horse in clay. Its head stood twenty-four feet tall. He intended to finish the sculpture in bronze, but in 1494, French soldiers invaded his home in Italy. Their attack accomplished its goal, and the French destroyed da Vinci's horse as a way to humiliate the people they had defeated. For the rest of his days, da Vinci mourned the loss of the sculpture.

⁂

Wyoming winters wear on you. Weather reduces the landscape to a monochrome array of white, interrupted, on occasion, by the silhouettes of trees. It's the palette of gray that moved Lynn and me to plan a visit to the wild horse sanctuary in the Black Hills. We needed a getaway, although we hoped it might turn into more. We wanted to see a swath of color: paints, pintos, and Appaloosas. We booked the bunkhouse on Hyde's ranch and planned a trip around a forecast for snow. On the radar, it looked like we could drive to Hot Springs before the weather started. It seemed like we could hole up in the bunkhouse for a night, and then head back to Wyoming after the front had passed. When we set out, we did not know the snow would turn into a storm.

We arrive at the sanctuary in the afternoon under a sky inset with scattered clouds. It only takes a moment to check into the bunk and unload our car. That leaves us with an hour of sunlight. The bunkhouse stands next to a pasture where sanctuary staff observe new horses before turning them loose on the property. We bundle up and walk over to the fence line.

In the fall, the BLM had removed several bands of wild horses from a region of Wyoming called Adobe Town, an area of khaki cliffs and globular rock formations. In the weeks that followed, one of the bands received notoriety in photos and stories posted on the internet. Horse advocates named the band's stallion "Bronze Warrior." People admired him for his color and his muscular appearance. After the BLM removed Bronze Warrior from his home, wild horse supporters went to work looking for a way to free his family from their sentence in a long-term holding pen. Carol Walker, a

Colorado-based photographer, approached the staff at Dayton Hyde's sanctuary. They found room for Bronze Warrior and his band in the Black Hills.

We recognize the stallion and his mares in the pasture next to the bunkhouse. In the past two months, they had been hazed by a helicopter, separated from each other, stored in a government facility, trucked across state lines, and then they were finally reunited. They look perfect against the backdrop of stone cliffs on the Cheyenne. Since we know Bronze Warrior's name, and because we know his story, seeing him gives us a reason to feel affirmed. In *Becoming Cousteau*, a documentary film, the late oceanographer Jacques Cousteau uses a phrase that's become a principle of conservation. With regard to landscapes, waterways, and animals, "you only protect what you love." As we came to know Bronze Warrior, we started to care about his fate.

When you spend time with horses, even wild ones, it's natural to give them names. How do we save our memories, and then share them with others, if the characters in the stories aren't named? We name everything. It's how we make sense of the world. When you see a band of mustangs on the prairie, even if it's a group you've never seen before, you give them a name in order to be able to talk or even think about them afterward. In the case of Bronze Warrior, having a name and story saved his life—the words and images inspired people to write emails and make phone calls. Bronze Warrior became a cause. Advocates worked until they found him a future in the sanctuary.

But there's another side—a darker side—to the act of giving names to wild animals and then caring about them. American life is marked by polarization. We affiliate with groups that look for ways to harm one another. Too often, if it becomes known that one group of people cares about something, that makes the thing into a target. Poachers shot one of the most well-known horses in Wyoming, a stallion by the name of Desert Dust. The animal appeared in a film, and artists painted his likeness. Drive-by shooters took his life in a pasture outside the home of the rancher and wild horse supporter, Frank Robbins.

In the 2000s, a bull elk took up residence in Estes Park, Colorado. Because of his size and heavily pointed rack, townspeople named him "Sampson." Facebook posts celebrated the animal's choice to live, comfortably and without fear, in Estes Park. A homeowner found Sampson decapitated. Similarly, on the outskirts of Juneau, Alaska, hikers noticed a wolf engaging dogs and people in playful interactions. The wolf seemed to look forward to the encounters. The thought of a friendly wolf thrilled Juneau residents. Nick Jans, a local author, called him "Romeo," and the name stuck. Tales of Romeo sightings were recounted and broadcast on a radio talk show. I don't have to tell you the end of the story. On the internet, and in letters to Alaska news outlets, one phrase appeared online with consistence: "The only good wolf is a dead wolf." Today, if a group of people love and name an animal, in effect, their feelings and actions place a bull's-eye on the creature's back. Somehow, nature became an arena where we fight a portion of our culture wars.

Ironically, during some of the most turbulent eras of American history, our leaders passed landmark environmental laws with broad bipartisan support. In the decades of the 1960s and 1970s, when civil rights, the fight for gender equality, and questions about our involvement in Vietnam roiled and split the nation into aggravated clans, we passed: the Wilderness Act, the Clean Air Act, the Clean Water Act, the Endangered Species Act, and the Wild and Free-Roaming Horses and Burros Act as well. All of the acts passed with backing from congresspeople across party lines. Historically, when we have found ourselves divided over hotly contested issues—clean air, safe water, and the protection of needful creatures gave people a common cause. Today, the preservation of landscapes and animals no longer provides us with a mutual set of goals. Recently, in the parking lot of a grocery store, I walked past a bumper sticker on a pickup truck. It said, "Tree-Huggers Suck."

After sunset, Lynn and I retire to the bunkhouse. We climb into bed with books and fall asleep to the sound of wind-driven snow tapping the metal roof. In the morning, when I open my eyes, my first sight includes a drift of snow that blew in from a crack under the door. That makes me curious. I go to the window and discover that a white dune swallowed our car. I see the roofline of the Subaru, but that is all I see. Overnight, the weather turned into an event called Winter Storm Europa—two feet of snow and forty-five-mile-per-hour wind.

After coffee, I put on boots and hike to the IRAM office. I explain that our car is buried. I ask, "Do you have someone to plow us out?" The woman on staff explains that the sanctuary only has two hands in the winter: the ranch manager, Dave, and a man named Rick, a summer volunteer who they convinced to stay. She says, "They have to feed the horses first." She explains that many of the horses at the sanctuary can no longer forage on their own, so each day the crew delivers hay and nutritional pellets to a set of places on the property.

I say, "Of course. We'll wait."

The bunkhouse comes stocked with a stack of John Wayne movie discs. We watch *Rio Bravo* over breakfast. Then we spend an hour looking out the window at snow blowing off the tops of drifts, growing in height across the valley. After lunch, we watch *True Grit* and I fall asleep to *The Sons of Katy Elder* in the afternoon. Before dinner, well after checkout time, I call the office.

I ask, "Any chance that Dave or Rick can plow us out?"

She says, "No. They haven't come back from feeding." Then she asks me if tomorrow is too late.

I look at Lynn with my hand covering the phone. I whisper, "*Tomorrow.*" Then I ask, "Can we stay one more night?"

She says, "All we have left to eat is chili. Can you eat chili again?" Then she adds, "Can you eat chili for breakfast?"

I love chili, so I lift my hand off of the phone and tell the office, "That sounds good. We'll look for somebody to plow us out tomorrow."

"Yeah. I'll send Dave over with the tractor after horses have been fed. They'll get started at eight. With luck, they'll finish before lunch."

Tonight's feature film is *Rooster Cogburn*, starring: John Wayne.

With the electric baseboard heater set on high, we can keep the bunkhouse at about fifty degrees. Lynn travels with extra blankets, though. We survive the night at the bottom of a pile of fabric.

In the morning, I use a dustpan to scrape up the snow blown in from underneath the door. At the window, I notice the sky is clear. The wind is still blowing, but a piece of blue sky also looms cheerfully overhead.

After coffee and a cup of chili, Lynn and I stare at each other. I walk over to the cabinet below the television set. I grab a John Wayne movie called *McClintock!*, then I walk it back to the kitchen and tilt it toward Lynn. I raise my eyebrows in an encouraging way. My wife says, "No." Now we have to think about how to spend the day.

I say, "Maybe we should make ourselves useful." I tell Lynn, "We should give Dave and Rick a hand feeding horses."

She looks out the window of the bunkhouse at the outbuildings. One of the pickups is running and we see a tractor heading toward a bale of hay.

When we travel in the wintertime, I pack boots, gloves, and hats. Then I pack extra coats and mittens too. At the door of the bunkhouse, I pull on my boots and throw a scarf around my neck. Lynn says, "See if you can catch them."

I find Rick in one of the outbuildings. He's looking for a scraper. A film of ice covered the windshield of the truck left outside overnight. Neither of us find a real scraper, but I pick up a yardstick and give it to him.

He takes the stick and says, "That ought to work."

On our way to the truck, I ask, "Can we give you a hand feeding horses?"

"It's pretty cold. The storm is over. But it's cold."

I hold up my wool-lined leather mittens. Then I point one of them at my boots in a gesture that says, "No problem."

"Ok. That'd be nice if you want to help."

I say, "Lynn's getting ready." Then I ask, "Can we pick her up at the bunkhouse?"

"Alright."

⁘⁖⁘⁖⁘

We're riding in a pickup outfitted with a grain hopper in back. After introductions, Rick takes a minute to explain that he and Dave drive similar routes in the morning. Dave uses a tractor to drop hay at a set of preselected spots. Rick follows behind in the truck. Once a line of hay is on the ground, he drives beside the row. He pushes a button on the dashboard, and then the hopper in the back releases pellets as the pickup rolls along.

We drive up the road away from the bunkhouse. Then we turn right. I hop out to open a gate, and we continue on what looks like it might have been a two-track Jeep path, somewhere under all the snow. The terrain undulates between ridges and bottomlands. Out ahead, we see Dave on the lower portion of a hollow. The tractor pulls an implement that busts hay bales and lays the loose forage onto the ground.

We plod our way through drifts, heading toward the bottom of the draw. Through the window of the truck, I see horses streaming from the hilltops. Mustangs move in rows, coming through the snow on lines they make by walking one by one. Horses and trails write a pattern onto the slopes, and the forms strike me as artful.

⁘⁖⁘⁖⁘

Klaus Hupert, a researcher at the University of Stuttgart, describes paths that animals create as "desire lines." Forests and prairies are full of them. In Japan, they call them "beast trails." In France, they refer to them as "donkey paths," and when we give thought to them in the United States, we usually describe them as "game trails."

Over the course of our lives, we grow accustomed to moving through communities organized into grids—city blocks and numbered streets. Our paths rarely follow the contours of our landscapes or the shape of our desire. When we travel through the streets of home, our routes reflect the models held in the minds of civil engineers. In the developed world, the rectangle grew to become our shape of choice. Rectangular grids suit our fondness for rectangular homes and offices, but our grids also separate our longings from the curves, reliefs, and watersheds that define our habitats.

In contrast, when horses set desire lines in the soil or snow, they do so as a response to their wishes and the terrain. In *The Art of the Commonplace*, Wendell Berry suggests the paths created by creatures represent "the perfect adaptation ... of movement to place." When horses approach a valley, the hillsides offer them an infinite set of possibilities. Just by walking, they shrink an ocean of options down to a single route—a riverbed that pulses with a current of motion. In the time that it takes for us to catch up to Dave in the tractor, I enjoy the view of horses winding down the slopes.

When we arrive at the bottom of the valley, seventy horses stand in line, gobbling hay. At the sound of the pickup, some of them lift their heads. The pellets we're hauling contain a tasty blend of corn and molasses. Rick lines up the truck beside the hay, but before he opens the hopper, he says, "Why don't you two go out and mingle." Lynn and I climb from the cab, and we find ourselves surrounded.

I am accustomed to watching wild mustangs on the Wyoming prairie. In our home state, if you are quiet, and if you move slow, a band might let you walk up within fifty or sixty feet of them. In this case, horses brush past our elbows. They nudge us with heavy shoulders. Some of them turn their heads and look us in the eye.

I've spent a good deal of my life in the outdoors—fishing, hiking, biking, skiing, and watching wildlife. I added "spending time with wild horses" to my list of pursuits for some obvious reasons: they are stunning to look at, and the places where they tend to live are lovely too. Most animals possess aesthetic qualities however, and when it comes to the landscapes and waterways of the West, the scenery is on your side, no matter where you look. Still, the experience of watching bands of wild horses differs from other forms of interaction with the animal kingdom. In most of nature, when a person finds or comes across a wild creature, the encounters are brief and often distinguished by either nonchalance or fear on the part of the animal.

I've never been able to spend more than about five seconds in the presence of a coyote, for example. In most of the West, they've learned to feel afraid of people. In my past, I fly fished at a level of frequency that bordered on obsession. Trout are gorgeous, but when you catch one, it becomes clear that they would rather you left them alone. I enjoy bird-watching too, but most of the time, when I look at birds and our eyes meet, I feel a coolness in their glance. On the other hand, when you look at horses, they look back. They're curious. Elk and antelope will usually run from the sight of a human, but when I spend time on the prairie with mustangs, I am left with the sense that their interest in me matches my wonder at their existence.

Through the morning, we make four more stops with hay and pellets. On each occasion, when they see the truck, horses start to press their way through the snow toward a meal. To pass the time, I count the mustangs at each interval. By the end of the route, I estimate that we fed 400 animals, but from brochures in the bunkhouse I learned that the sanctuary is home to more than 500.

I ask Rick, "Is that all of the horses?"

"No. There are a hundred or so that we don't feed."

"Why not?"

"They're too wild. When we turn them loose, they cross the Cheyenne River and then climb through canyons to the top of the ridge. That's where they stay—on the side of the river opposite the ranch. Sometimes we see them on top of the cliffs. Once in a while, they come back to the river to drink, but they don't come all the way back." Rick points to the ridge above the river and says, "They live up there."

I am confused. I start to think out loud, "They can come down from the hills above the river any time? They can follow a routine, eat hay and pellets every morning, and live the good life, but they don't?"

"Yeah. They don't want hay or pellets or people. There's enough food and water on the other side of the river. It's tougher over there. But they don't want an easy life. They want freedom, like they had before the government sentenced them to life in a holding pen. They are wild, and we have room. If it's freedom they want, they can have that." When Rick finishes the explanation, it is quiet in the truck. The three of us are thinking about wildness.

⸙ ▾ ▴ ⸙ ▾ ▴ ⸙

As human beings, and as Americans, we tether our lives to agendas, calendars, and bundles of obligations. We tie our days to the clock and the goals we expect to achieve. After Rick told us about the horses that preserve their wildness on the other side of the river, I started to think about how I felt when I realized we were not going home according to plan. When I found out we were stranded, I started to think about all the things I wasn't going to be able to do on account of Winter Storm Europa and having to spend an extra day in the bunkhouse. The fear of "lost time" gripped my attention.

We see time, and just about everything else, as a type of currency—something to spend or lose—something to covet as a means to something else, like funds in a bank account. These thought patterns, and the pursuits that flow from them, have the effect of binding our will. In a book called *The Social Contract*, Jean-Jacques Rousseau said, "Man is born free and everywhere he is in chains." The chains are made of expectations, personal and cultural. We inherit some, and then over the course of a life we create more, and more are built on our behalf, link by link until we're bound.

We drop Lynn off at the bunkhouse when we're finished with the chores. I ride with Rick back to the spot where he parks the pickup. I give him a hand unloading tools. Then I walk back to the bunk to rejoin Lynn. From the road, I can see that Dave has cleared a path out of the parking lot. It runs from our car up the hill and out of sight.

As I walk along, I notice something. A horse stands at the top of the ridge. It's a palomino stallion on the high side of the river, and he's looking down at me. In the horse's stare, I feel myself become the focal point within his field of vision.

When people look at each other, the land, and animals, we use our eyes to take their measure. There is power in our gaze, but in this moment, I feel the stallion assessing me. My world is pressed down upon me by the eyes of the horse: my hat, my coat, my boots on the road, my past, my plans, conceits, and insecurities. I begin to see myself through the eyes of the animal. Ralph Waldo Emerson suggested, "Dreams and beasts are two keys by which we are to find out the secrets of our nature." Our dreams serve as demonstrations of what we can become. For better and for worse, wild creatures show us what we're not. For all the value that we place on freedom, are we free?

When I make it back to the bunkhouse, I am excited to report that I saw a horse on the wild side of the river. Lynn and I look out the window through binoculars, but we can't find the stallion.

I say, "I saw a horse. Right there."

With her eyes still pinned to the distance, Lynn says quietly, "He saw you too."

Then she pauses and turns to look at me.

"He's gone."

THE HORSE WITH A THOUSAND NAMES

The universe is made of stories, not of atoms.

—Muriel Rukheyser, *The Speed of Darkness*

To be human is to be linguistically . . . enframed.

—Max Oelschlager, *The Idea of Wilderness*

hen you live in Wyoming, you feel the gravity of the National Parks. They tug on your attention. For the first decade that Lynn and I lived in Casper, we spent our spare time together in Yellowstone and Grand Teton. On route from our house to the northwest corner of the state, we drove along the edge of Green Mountain. Each time we passed its peaks, Lynn would say things like, "We should drive up there someday." I would reply, "Yeah. I could fly fish." A decade into our tenure as residents of Wyoming, we finally found out about wild horses, but I hadn't yet given up on clear-running streams and trout.

When a free weekend showed up on our schedule, we packed a tent and made Green Mountain our destination. I intended to fish the creek that runs from the high country to the plains at the base of the range. Lynn planned to pick sagebrush. She likes to wrap and bundle the branches. We weren't aware that Green Mountain served as a home for a herd of mustangs. We associated wild horses with the Red Desert and the prairies of our home state. We didn't know it yet, but we were poised to make another discovery.

Two miles from the site where we planned to set up camp, we notice a sign on the side of the road. In brown and white it says, "Cottonwood Campground—2 miles." The next line says, "Wild Horse Point—10 miles." The arrows lead in the same direction. We look at each other. Lynn says what we are both thinking, "Wild horses?" We pitch the tent beside Cottonwood Creek. Then we take a minute to open a couple of beers. It's a tradition. We drink a brew when we christen a new campsite. We unfold our collapsible chairs and gather a bunch of firewood. I consider fishing, but the thought of wild horses keeps me off the water. I ask, "Do you think there are mustangs on this mountain?" Lynn says, "I don't know. Let's drive up and take a look."

It's an uneven path that leads to the top of the range. It switchbacks through stands of pine to an elevation of 8,600 feet. At the top, the trees thin out. The road runs beside the rim of a ledge that offers a view of the Red Desert stretching toward the south. At the summit, another sign directs us to the east. We plunk between ruts on the trail for a mile and then stop at a parking lot. Wild Horse Point hosts a picnic ground with a long view.

We store a pair of binoculars in the backseat of our station wagon. We use them to look for owls, but this time we train the glass on a row of dots in the distance. They look like horses, but they're too far off. I cannot tell. They could be cows, but it's still fun to stare into the panorama.

After we're satisfied that there are no mustangs at Wild Horse Point, we climb back in the car. Instead of driving back to camp, we take a left on a road that winds through a meadow. Lynn admires the blue-green sage. I notice something, though. I see a patch of gold and white. It's the back of a mustang. My instincts shoot my right foot to the brake pedal. The car lurches and Lynn says, "What?" so I point out through my window. Then we grab our cameras. We start to walk, slowly, through the brush toward the horse. He's grazing in a gully. The sound of tires on gravel alerted him to our presence, so when we appear over the crest of the ridge, he's not surprised. He looks at us and then lowers his head. He returns to eating.

Once we have hiked enough to take a good look at the horse, we see that he's not alone. He is standing in the shadow of four other mustangs—a band of bachelors—gray and black males spending the summer at the top of the mountain. They coordinate their grazing. Heads shift from side to side, between bunches of grass. We hedge up to the gold and white horse. We move closer. Then he takes a step to maintain his distance. Lynn and I notice, when he walks away, the others also readjust. They shift to separate themselves from him.

Lynn says, "He's an outsider. They won't let him join the group."

I ask, "Do you want to loop around and try to move in closer to the bachelors?"

"No," she answers. Then she says, "I want to stay with Pony-boy."

Lynn didn't have to think long about what to call the horse. She blurted his name like it was something that she'd always known. At this point, we'd only just started into lives devoted to wild horse travel, image-making, and advocacy work. We hadn't formally given names to any mustangs yet, at least, no names outside of "bay stallion" or the "little black and white pinto."

In the years prior to our discovery of wild horses, we'd spent a long time observing and making photographs of other types of animals: elk, deer, and bison. We had never named any of them. In Yellowstone, for example, grizzly bears each have a number. We used to search the park looking for Bear 399. Numbers don't lend themselves to narrative. It's tough to build a meaningful story about a number. On the other hand, the name "Ponyboy" stirs our imaginations. We talk about the character by that name in the film *The Outsiders*, based on the book by S. E. Hinton. We wonder if the painted horse had been marginalized on account of his two-toned gold and white coat. We ponder the question of whether horses can feel excluded. We start to build Ponyboy's past. We begin to weave him a biography. We cannot help ourselves.

Other creatures engage the world by different means. Ospreys absorb the ground with their vision, for example. They interpret their habitat with their two eyes. Badgers live in dark and quiet haunts. They depend on their sense of touch—feeling their way through rocks and bones under the surface of the earth. A grizzly bear can smell food four miles away, but we don't work like that. During the course of human evolution, our senses lost acuteness. We cannot see or smell or hear like other animals. Our senses provide our brains with a simple baseline of information. Upon that line, our minds go to work assembling words. We use words to give meaning to places and events. For example, when I look out my living room window onto my lawn, I see "dandelions." The word defines my experience of the "weeds" in my front yard. "Dandelions" are "weeds."

When you walk through the lawn "care" aisle of a hardware store, you smell the herbicide. Pesticide. Mists and sprays and bags of granules. We must eradicate the weeds. If we fail, it becomes a commentary on our character. Dandelions in the yard serve as a sign—an indication of negligence. When homeowners allow dandelions onto the lawn, it means that they don't care about the value of their real estate. Even worse, it could mean that they don't care about the value of their neighbor's property.

In some nations, when they speak of "values," they invoke a set of principles. For some, values represent the goals and standards that they work to live up to or embody. The Sioux value commitment to community. The Navajo value beauty in their lives and in the world, but when Americans use the word "value," we rarely refer to standards or principles. More often, we use the term to refer to the cost of goods or services. Our tendency is to reduce our understanding of both our environment and ourselves to prices set in the market. For example, when our superiors set our annual salaries, they put a price tag on a year's worth of our days. After work, we go home to our largest investment, or largest expense, our house. The story that we use to understand life is the story of economics.

It's a potent story. When the first wave of Americans made their way out of the eastern forests and onto the grasslands of the West, we found the largest mass of migrating mammals ever known: bison. We also found an array of plants and animals living in concert with the herds, a complement of flora and fauna richer and more diverse than any that we are aware of historically. We didn't see the western prairie as a miracle of nature, however. We saw parcels of real estate. We saw the soil as property and the grass as a means to grow commodities. Cattle, mostly. The narrative we used to explain what we found centered on finance. In our culture, we leave little room for moral and aesthetic considerations. We don't dwell on questions of truth or rightness or beauty. Our story demands that we use "resources" to contribute to economic growth.

In the beginning, grizzly bears lived on the prairie. The marketplace does not value grizzlies. Plus, they are big and dangerous. We killed them first. Then we removed the wolves. Afterward, we turned a herd of up to 60 million bison into a group of 23 animals. We placed bounties on the heads of coyotes and mountain lions. We poisoned the prairie dog. When prairie dog towns disappeared, we lost the predators that depend on them: burrowing owls and black-footed ferrets. In short, we turned the wildest region on earth—the Great Plains—into an enormous, one dimensional, mono-cultural, veal-fattening pen. We created "flyover country," the geographical equivalent of a factory floor.

We're taught to picture trees and mountains when we picture "wilderness." The official wilderness areas protected by the government contain either forests or mountain peaks. I've visited many of the wilderness areas in the West. The weather is wild. Straight-line winds tear at the fabric of tents. Sometimes, in the middle of a storm, it sounds like you're stuck in the same room as lightning. Most animals know better than to dwell in places covered by snow for a large part of the year, however. Our wilderness areas are pretty, but the land is often barren. Wilderness areas rarely provide homes for large or diverse collections of animals. Some wilderness areas consist solely of rock and ice. Rock and ice possess no economic value, so when politicians went to designate wild places "untrammeled by man," they had the tops of mountain ranges to choose from. Since we found ways to make money on grasslands, we trammeled them thoroughly, but in the past, prairies were ferocious. The Great Plains were the wildest places on the planet.

Not long after Lynn and I discovered that there were wild horses in Wyoming, we learned that the term "wild" is not universally used to describe them. In Wyoming, and other states with herds of mustangs, organized groups are fighting to remove the word "wild" from conversations about horses. In particular, agribusiness people who graze cattle on public land want the term "wild" removed from our vocabulary. They prefer the word "feral." In English, we define the terms similarly. Synonyms for both include "savage," "untamed," and "undomesticated." But the connotations of the words differ. We use "wild" to suggest a state of freedom and originality. In contrast, we use the term "feral" to describe domestic animals that have escaped.

The term "wild" conjures romantic feelings in our culture. When we see wild animals through the windows of our cars, we're often thrilled. We'll pull off of a road and stop to admire a wild animal. We make photographs and post them on the internet. As a resident of Wyoming, I can attest: people travel for thousands of miles to drive the roads of my home state, just for the chance to *maybe* see something wild. The term feral does not move us that way. We don't plan summer vacations around feral animals. With regard to the feral—we feel disdain.

Animals are animals. Even so, some we like and some we don't. We take naps with some of them on the couch. Some we butcher and eat. We love German shepherds, but we built a federal office charged with trapping, poisoning, and blowing up the dens of coyotes. We snuggle with huskies, but in most of Wyoming, anyone can shoot a wolf on sight. Scholars have only recently begun to give attention to the significance that we attach to animals. In contrast, social scientists have spent years giving thought to the ways that we treat each other. Sociologists have spent a century trying to understand the relationships that form between groups of people. Among those who study such relations, the work of Gordon Allport stands out as distinctive. In his book *The Nature of Prejudice*, he describes the processes that lead to bigotry.

Allport suggests that our first contact with a group can shape our attitudes toward them for generations. His theory hinges on the power or status of people when they meet one another for the first time. Allport's model predicts that two different cultures will enjoy respectful relations when their first contact occurs at a time when they are equal. On the other hand, when groups of what people consider "unequal status" meet, the encounter results in racism, or a scenario where the dominant faction fails to accept the humanity of the other. Of course, such views provide the make-believe justification for wars, imperialism, and enslavement.

When we see horses for the first time, it is nearly always in the context of a domestic setting. They pull our carts, buggies, and handsome cabs. Sometimes, we cinch a saddle on their backs and we ask them to carry us. We come to know horses as property, although most of us will never possess the land or resources needed to keep them. However, for many in the West, particularly those who own horses, free roaming mustangs represent a threat to the established order. Westerners often see wild horses as having moved up beyond their station. This point of view can breed contempt. Many in the West look at mustangs with the same sort of condescension that we usually reserve for barnyard animals that manage to escape the farm.

It should come as no surprise to find stock growers working to change the way we talk about wild horses. The word "feral" reduces the romanticism and admiration that we feel toward mustangs. From the standpoint of those who use our public lands for their own personal profit, the foals of wild horses appear on the prairie as weeds. They are "unproductive." In the minds of many ranchers, mustangs deserve the same kind of disrespect that we apply to dandelions sprouting uninvited on suburban lawns. The wild horses that roam free in the West have never known owners or domesticity. Even so, lobbyists for agribusinesses have begun a campaign to define the American mustang as a "feral" animal. If they succeed, it is conceivable that horses would suffer the same fate that we prescribe for other animals that we refer to as feral: poison, traps, and bullets.

Agribusiness people have an economic agenda. They look at the public grasslands of the West through a lens shaped by the workings of the marketplace. When it comes to the prairie landscapes that belong to all of us, in permanence, they tend to see monthly allotments of food for their own private herds.

The language of economics animates the stories that we tell about the western states. The market that provides us with goods and services shapes our worldview to such a degree, the practice of reducing everything to economics can feel inevitable. But within the scope of history, the market-based approach to life is relatively new. Historically, human beings tempered the judgments that take place in the market with folklore. In the past, we used legends and myths to provide members of society with lessons, ethics, morals, and aesthetic preferences. Cultural narratives offered a way for human beings to reduce the intensity of our obsession with finances. Folktales and parables allowed people to sidestep concerns about what is profitable in order to focus on questions like, "How should we live?" or "Where lies the truth?" or "When is something beautiful?"

During the time of their empire, Greeks found so much meaning in horses that they began to imagine a race of creatures that combined the body of a horse with the torso of a man: the centaur. Greeks valued the freedom of wild horses. Observing the beasts gave them a reason to consider the contrast between the willfulness of nature and the constraints we feel as members of societies. Centaurs possessed the traits of both horse and man, but their character leaned toward that of the animal. In Greek mythology, centaurs appear feisty and spirited. That is, with one exception—the centaur Chiron—brother of Zeus and the tutor of Achilles. For the Greeks, Chiron represented patience, skill, and kindness. He served as a role model for those who would later become physicians. Myths and allegories serve the function of helping people to entertain the promise of a better world. For ages, horses have been a part of that promise.

As societies like ours evolved, we used the science and economics stories to banish our other narratives. Even so, for most of American history, horse stories gave us meaning. In the middle of the last century, we used horses as characters to help us define who we are, but we're two generations removed from culture-forming films like *My Friend Flicka* and *The Black Stallion*. The romance has waned. We now use cold calculations to provide the rationale for removing wild horses from public land. We're left with the hollow characterization of the prairie as a commercial landscape. At times, it can feel like we are caught in a Greek tragedy. In the production of a tragedy, a principle is set in motion. Then the principle plays itself out—all the way out—despite the efforts of those who understand the plot leads downward to a melancholy end.

Lynn and I watched Ponyboy, off and on, for seven months. He stayed in the margins. We'd find him eating grass twenty feet from a group of bachelor stallions. Then, one day, we found the group that he tended to lurk near, but no Ponyboy. Through the winter, and into spring, Lynn and I would ask each other, "Where is Pony?" It became a meme. Now it's been years since we've seen the gold and white horse, but we still ask each other, "Where is Ponyboy?" It makes me wonder where he went. I also wonder how many other people knew the horse. It makes me curious about the names they might have given him. The last time we saw Pony, he had grown accustomed to cars on the road through his favorite meadow. He might have a thousand other names.

Much has been written about the Adopt-a-Mustang program sponsored by the Bureau of Land Management. It's a good program. Or, at least, a necessary one. Adoption is a better fate than a glue factory for horses that threaten to eat the grass that a small number of us would rather feed to cows and calves. Government agents round up the horses that they find. Then they offer them to potential owners, for a modest charge. Of course, in the arrangement, wild horses become property. They are broken. Although we like to say that they are "gentled."

Mustang trainers will repeat a horse's name until the animals develop new identities. Horses are smart. You don't have to echo their names too often before they start to recognize them. Knowing one's name is the first step toward taking on all of the obligations that go along with being somebody. "Buttercup," for example. If you can get a horse to accept the name, that is the first step toward getting them to fulfill the responsibilities involved in being Buttercup.

Buttercup holds still for a halter.
Buttercup stands quietly in her stall.
Buttercup walks into the barn to eat her grain.
And so on, in an effort toward domestication.

Having a name is like having a job. Ponyboy may have a thousand names, but the lucky horse does not know one of them.

⁂

Lynn and I keep planning new trips into the sagebrush. Part of me hopes to find Pony. There is also part of me that hopes he's hiding somewhere in a valley or a canyon, out of reach—far from tourists and government officials. Near the end of the film *The Outsiders*, the character Johnny says something to the namesake of the horse that we met at the top of Green Mountain. He borrows a line from a poem by Robert Frost. He whispers, "Stay gold, Ponyboy. Stay gold."

FINDING REVERENCE IN ROOSEVELT

Teddy . . . seemed to burn more brightly and live more fully than others, savoring every detail and every challenge.

—Christopher Knowlton, *Cattle Kingdom*

Lynn judges my enthusiasm for a travel destination by taking stock of the time I spend reading its history. Sometimes, I read about a place before I visit. Other times, if I am struck by a location, I read about it afterward. In the case of Theodore Roosevelt National Park, I read about the setting before we left for North Dakota, I kept on while we were there, and then I continued after we went home. Our original interest in the area arose when we discovered that Theodore Roosevelt is the only park in the United States that plays host to bands of wild horses. That alone seemed like a good reason to plan a trip. Only later did I see that the outing would spark a year's worth of thought about wildness, prairies, and the power of one person to change the way that people think about the world.

⁙⁘⁙ ⁘⁙

We arrive in the village of Medora after dark. The rooftops of old-time buildings form a line, strung out like boxcars on the horizon. We pull into a gas station on the main street. After I fill the tank, I join Lynn in the gift shop and convenience store. While she adds milk to a cup of tea, I wander through the aisles. Every shelf is full of souvenirs: t-shirts, mugs, shot glasses, and leather belts bejeweled with brightly colored beads. We're "traveling." Everything about the space we're in suggests that we are about to begin a vacation, or maybe even something closer to a pilgrimage in one of the nation's parks.

It's a throng of shapes and colors in the gift shop on Main Street in Medora, but I gravitate toward a shelf of books. Histories of North Dakota stand beside biographies of Roosevelt. I also find a guide to the bands of wild horses in the area. The book contains photos, names, and descriptions of well-known mares and stallions. I spend a moment reading about a silver horse named Arrowhead. He strikes me as a masterpiece of DNA: thick neck, broad shoulders, and a chiseled jaw. It's an engaging book, but it is expensive. We're on a budget, and we discovered, halfway to Medora, that we forgot our coffee cups. I notice that Lynn is waiting in the car, so I choose two Roosevelt mugs from a shelf.

With a full tank and a new pair of souvenirs, we pass through the guard station on the park's southern border. At night, the outlines of ridges and valleys only offer dark hints about the contour of the land. My imagination fills the shadows with sleeping bands of mustangs, resting nose to nose. It's a soothing image, but the night is black, it's getting late, and we are occupied with the thought of the campsite waiting for us on the Little Missouri. We make our way to the site without stopping to see what the darkness holds.

Cottonwood Camp sits at the bottom of a valley in a grove of trees. Our site enjoys the shelter of branches overhead, and it is close to the river too. We're able to listen to water lapping along the edge of the stream while we pitch our canvas teepee.

Lynn is tired. It has been a long day in the car, so we pour some red wine into our Roosevelt mugs and blow up our mattresses. With our bedding set, I say goodnight. I spent the decades of my twenties and thirties zealously fly fishing. I don't fish for trout much anymore, but I still feel an impulse to stand in rivers with the current washing over my knees. I refill my mug and walk to the water.

Three weeks prior to the trip, I started to read about Roosevelt. As president, he protected our first monument, Devil's Tower, and the nation's first park, Yellowstone. At a time when we busied ourselves cutting down forests, damming rivers, and strip mining for coal and copper, Roosevelt waged a policy war of opposition. He fought against what we think of as a simple march toward "progress." His primary weapon in the fight was his personality, coupled with everybody else's understanding of the legend—his life story.

Nations across the world and throughout time have given rise to wise and noteworthy people. Every culture finds a way to exalt its formidable characters. We called Roosevelt our 26th president. If he were alive in another time, or another place, they would have likely called him a shaman. As a tradition, shamanism extends backward through 30,000 years of history. It spanned the globe to include examples on every continent except Antarctica. The techniques of shamanism developed along similar lines, from one end of the earth to the other, despite the distance separating the practitioners. Apparently, across the globe and at key times, societies found a need for shamans.

Anthropologists have documented the steps most often taken in the process of elevating someone to such a status. In nearly every case, a would-be shaman suffers a crisis in the form of an illness or a shock. The woe they feel begins to separate them from others. Then the sorrow starts to move them, to the point where they set out from home. In some cultures, the journeys are physical. A budding shaman will travel, typically in solitude, in search of a vision. In other places, the passage is mystical. The voyage involves a trek into the spirit world. In either case, shamans return with a new set of skills. They also wear costumes as a way to indicate that they've been changed. Then they start to console people. They begin to counsel their communities.

On the evening of Valentine's Day, 1884, on different floors of his New York home, Theodore Roosevelt lost the two most beloved people in his world: his wife and his mother. By all accounts, the deaths left him in something akin to a trance. One of his associates was known to have said, in the weeks after the events, "He does not know what he does or says." In his journal, Roosevelt confessed, "The light went out of my life." He left for North Dakota, beyond the lands of Daniel Boone and Davy Crockett, to the West, where an American form of wildness endured.

Historians agree, the experience of moving to the plains impacted Roosevelt. He spent a year in a shack on the Little Missouri. In his words, with respect to the time that he gave to the prairie, "It is where the romance of my life began." Photos from the era offer a vision of Roosevelt having replaced his tailored three-piece suit with a buckskin leather one, rows of fringe across his shoulders, a bandana on his neck. The new attire served as a sign to observers. A transformation had occurred.

Roosevelt later returned to his home state of New York, and, of course, he spent a good deal of his days in Washington, DC. But he maintained a residence in North Dakota, a ranch upstream on the river. He returned to the western plains off and on throughout the rest of his life. He went for the adventure. The prairie served as a muse and a source of inspiration. Roosevelt used the solitude and solemnity of time spent in the out of doors to create a space in his mind, free from the ordinary norms and values of business and politics. He walked the path of a shaman. Like his predecessors, down through the ages, he lived on the borderland between two worlds. He used periods of separation from society, and immersion in nature, to expand his perceptions. Like a tribal shaman, Roosevelt used his time apart to build a platform of wisdom, from which he provided a contrast to commonly held, but wrongheaded, beliefs.

Historically, shamanism offered little in the way of actual medicine with healing properties. In the past, however, if a person approached a shaman with an illness or hardship, they expected to discover a new way to interpret the symptoms of the ailment. It turns out that stories are good medicine. When it comes to improvement in health, their effectiveness is well-established. The line of evidence in support of healing narratives begins with early anthropology and runs through contemporary studies of placebos conducted in medical schools. Perceptions are powerful. They hold the potential to heal, and to the degree that shamanism changes minds, the practice proves its worth. Even in a case where a death becomes imminent, a shaman can offer someone a new way to think about their fate.

Throughout history, individuals turned to shamans for the means to re-story and redefine themselves. Societies have done the same. In the end, shamanism serves a social role. Shamans use the things that set them apart—past suffering, travel, and appearance—to challenge the status quo when the behavior of a group begins to go awry. Their example throws back the curtain of culture that often limits our ability to make sensible choices. Shamans open up a place where people can give thought to what is possible.

In the time of Theodore Roosevelt, our once-proud frontier nation stood on the brink of becoming an urban and industrial land. The country found itself in the grip of a culture that hailed the captains of industry, while at the same time forsaking the landscapes that supported Indigenous people for thousands of years and later enchanted the country's settlers and colonists. This is the era of American history where we began to revel in the accumulation of wealth. We began to think of ourselves, primarily, as consumers. At the same time, Roosevelt gave us a new sense of our potential. Apart from his legislative victories, Roosevelt used the example of his life-in-the-outdoors to shift the way we think about our past, and more importantly, our futures.

Shamans offer us new stories, and every decent story is built around a string of expectations, left like breadcrumbs, running from the start to the end of a narrative. Stories employ the trick of anticipation. A good story inspires an expectant mood. The stories we told about Roosevelt's adventures in the West led a country hell-bent on covering its topography with railroads and smokestacks to see what we stood to lose if we left our course unchecked.

Roosevelt's example helped us to see the potential in wild places. He changed the way we see our habitat. In the words of another nineteenth-century shaman, Henry David Thoreau, "There is as much beauty in the landscape as we are prepared to appreciate." Thoreau went on to add, "We shall be fortunate … if we expect great things." Through the force of his biography and character, Roosevelt boosted our expectations. He challenged our culture of commerce and turned our hope to conservation.

In the morning, we drink coffee, eat cereal, and then climb in the car. When the United States government created the park, its directors paved a road meant to allow travelers to see a wide swath of the area in one circular route. Depending on the amount of time spent hiking, picnicking, and making photographs, visitors can plan to spend somewhere between a half day and a full day completing the circle drive.

Out on the road, I'm struck by the terrain. When settlers entered the western half of the Dakotas, they named their surroundings. They chose to describe them as "Badlands." Through their eyes, the setting radiated badness. Adjectives that authors included in writings on the place include "sparse," "barren," and "inhospitable," but they judged the West by standards set in the cultivated gardens of Europe and the East.

In contrast to the disappointment that settlers felt when they cast their eyes onto the valley of the Little Missouri, Roosevelt saw "a sacredness to the Badlands silhouette." He described the region as "so fantastically broken in form and so bizarre in color as to seem hardly properly to belong to this Earth." In his mind, the place "exuded a cosmic sense of God's Creation." As with other would-be shamans, Roosevelt needed a mythical place to build a new identity—a destination that would allow him to leave the confines of his prior self. To those ends, he found the Badlands abiding.

I stop at the first scenic lookout that we come upon. We're not alone in the parking lot. We pull in next to a station wagon at the end of a row of cars. Then we grab our cameras and make our way to a spot near a group of photographers. When we reach the other travelers-with-cameras, we discover that it's not the landscape that has drawn their attention. They're pointing their lenses at a group of prairie dogs.

I've lived in the West for three decades. This is the first full-fledged prairie dog town I have ever seen. When Lewis and Clark led the Corps of Discovery through the northern plains, prairie dogs appeared to them in "infinite" numbers. In fact, biologists speculate that the plains of the West were home to more than 5 billion prairie dogs as recently as a hundred years ago. One colony in Texas hosted 400 million residents. By the turn of the century, the number of black-tailed prairie dogs in the United States had been reduced by 98 percent. The population of the Gunnison's variety shrunk by 97 percent, and the white-tailed subspecies vanished from 92 percent of its former range.

Lynn and I join the photographers at the far end of the parking lot, and we start to observe. I don't know what I find more charming, the *yips* and *barks* of the prairie dogs or the *oohs* and *ahhs* coming from the group gathered to watch.

Prairie dogs form clans. They stand near the entrances to burrows and greet each other with hugs. Sometimes they kiss. The biologist Constantine Slobodchikoff notes, "They have the most sophisticated animal language decoded so far." We watch them chase each other back and forth across the colony. Then we marvel as they stop to clean each other's fur, but we press ahead because we're set on finding the wild horses in the park.

Back on the road, we roll in between hoodoos and down to the bottoms of glades. We watch a group of mule deer through the windows of the car. The pace of traffic slows at the top of a rise, and at first, we can't see why. Then we crest the ridge: a bull bison. The solitary beast stands on the summit, looking out through the folds and wrinkles stretching into the distance. A group of people stand at the road's edge holding cameras. We join them, quietly.

Lynn and I spend a lot of time in parks. One of the things that we like best are the people. National parks tend to bring out our most admirable traits. Inside a park, it seems, we are gracious. We practice humility. In our culture, the act of travel encourages us to pay homage to the places we visit. We go to locations that we value, and when we value a place, it shows in our eyes, our posture, and our actions.

Travelers rarely spray paint or shoot up road signs, for example. Local kids do that when they don't appreciate their surroundings—when they're missing reverence. Even beautiful places start to lose their luster when seen through the lens of our everyday lives as consumers and users of technology. When young people grow up unenthused, and the adults in their orbit allow them to take their habitat for granted, it can lead to a landscape becoming an object of scorn, a target for vandals. With regard to the management of parks and public land, we often assert "local control." But I would argue that locals aren't always the best stewards of their surroundings. We often grow desensitized to grandeur when we spend each day in its presence. Locals don't always adore their settings in the same manner as those who save vacation days and plan for years to see a place.

Theodore Roosevelt hunted bison, but by the late 1800s, the great herds had disappeared. Thus, on the occasions when Roosevelt could locate small groups of buffalo, he found it a moral challenge to shoot them. Like their cousins, prairie dogs, bison were seen as a financial threat to agribusiness people with a tendency to see our public grass-lands as their own private pastures. As a nation, both then and now, we place the interests of commerce ahead of ecology. "The chief business of the American people is business," said another United States president, Calvin Coolidge.

Roosevelt's path allowed him to see with a different pair of eyes. He saw through the veil that too often blinds us to anything but profit-making. In a biography of Roosevelt entitled *Wilderness Warrior*, the historian Douglas Brinkley explains how: "It sickened him to see wild ungulates being poisoned and slaughtered because they supposedly ate the same grass as cattle and sheep." In part, Roosevelt created Yellowstone National Park to preserve the last re-maining examples of wild bison left in the United States.

We don't approach the bull at the top of the ridge. We're not looking for close-ups. Lynn and I hold back and make photographs that include the animal as a part of the landscape. That's a difficult proposition, though. We have to time our exposures in concert with a photographer making circles around the bull at a distance that strikes us as too close. Bison are stoic. They are not known for their animate gestures. When they're not eating, they stand around. For travelers unfamiliar with bison behavior, the statue-like demeanor can mislead. When humans enter natural habitats, for the most part, other living things scatter when they see us. Not so with a bison bull. They stand there, unwavering. They don't even think to leave. As a result, they seem friendly, but they are not. In Yellowstone, bison injure more visitors than wolves, bears, and mountain lions combined. Because they don't run away, people walk up too close to them. Then, by the time they discover they made a mistake, it is too late. It's the indifference to threat that makes buffalo dangerous. Ironically, that trait also led to their demise. Bison hunters do not have to "hunt" them at all. They just walk up and shoot.

I put my camera down, but I cannot stop looking. I am struck by the image of the bull against a backdrop of rippling plains. Bison are relative newcomers to North America. Animals like horses and coyotes evolved here on this continent, over the course of more than 50 million years. In contrast, bison trace their original stock back to the Middle East. They are descendants of the great aurochs—the wild bovines that inhabited North Africa. Like human beings, bison migrated across Asia and into Alaska during the time of the last ice age. Bison did not evolve in North America, but this is their home. No one who sees them here could argue that they don't belong.

For our part, we press on and finish the drive. Any time we see a vantage point with uninterrupted views, we stop. Each occasion gives us a reason to step out of the car. We survey the land because the terrain is worth pausing to admire, but we're still on the lookout for mustangs. In the end the search is fruitless, however. We complete the circle and drive to the campground without sight of any horses.

⁂

After dinner, we decide to hike along the banks of the Little Missouri. Early on, we meet a ranger, and we stop to talk. We tell her we spent the day looking for horses, with no sign. She asks a handful of questions about the timing of our route. She explains how, over the years, she built a feel for the way horses move through the area, and then she makes a suggestion. She tells us to wake up early and drive toward the north. Her advice is to try to reach Jones Creek before sunup.

In the morning, we discover the value in a ranger's knowledge of a park. When we drive over the last crest separating us from Jones Creek, we are greeted by the sight of horses grazing at the bottom of a draw. We find two bands wading in the grass—not too far from the pavement. Then, as we drive closer, we see a band of six on a bald ridge, each wild horse striking a pose.

We're not the first to notice the mustangs. We pull onto the shoulder next to a pickup from Texas and a sedan with license plates from Michigan. The others are already making photos of the two bands enjoying a breakfast of little bluestem at the bottom of the valley. Both families of mustangs attempt to shield their foals. Mares position themselves between the photographers and their young ones.

The stallions stay to the side. They leave space between themselves and the others in order to monitor the scene.

Human beings and wolves and primates and elephants are among the only land mammals that create families and form attachments to each other like we find in the equine world. Horses build long-lasting and profound relationships. At a distance, you can often distinguish horses from other ungulates because they stand so close together that they touch. Cattle don't hug each other like that. Neither do elk or deer. Mustangs engage in friendly sparring games on their hind legs, they pull their friend's tails as a way to tease them, and they watch each other play in puddles after rain. They also hold established roles within their families. Mares and stallions posture themselves in relation to one another, their young, and the members of other bands. We know a lot about the social lives of horses, but our understanding of the animals is also limited.

Research on mustang behavior has been stunted by the status of the horse in our culture, and by the way we organize knowledge in universities. We tend to study animals in two places on an American campus, colleges of agriculture and departments of biology. Horses often become the subjects of scholars working in agriculture, but those researchers study domestic animals. They focus on husbandry and techniques for training horses as our servants. They overlook the wild ones. Similarly, in departments where they study fish and game, they also tend to ignore the behavior of horses, because we usually define them as property. In other words, mustangs fall between two established, but self-limiting fields. People who conduct research on domestic animals disregard them because they are not domestic, and people who study wildlife discount them because they don't consider them wildlife.

As a consequence, the workings of wild horse families, and much about the mind of *Equus*, remain enigmatic. The disciplines of biology and agriculture have provided an important baseline of knowledge with respect to horses, but neither field is situated to advance the cause. New insights will need to come from researchers in anthropology. As examples, both Jane Goodall and Diane Fossey studied primates under the guidance of the anthropologist Louis Leakey. They used the techniques of social science to break open our understanding of chimpanzees and gorillas.

The communal nature of horse life demands a new approach toward analysis, an approach that takes into account what it means to be a member of mustang society. In *Beyond Words: What Animals Think and Feel*, Carl Safina describes some of the considerations that social mammals need to make on a routine basis: "You have to keep track of specific individuals that you meet repeatedly, who might want your food or your mate or your rank and who might plot against you, or might plot with you against your rivals, or be there for you when it matters." He goes on to make an astute series of suggestions, with regard to the nature of the cognitive abilities we find in social species. Safina explains, "When individuals matter— when you're a 'who'—you need a social brain capable of reasoning, planning, rewarding, punishing, seducing, protecting, bonding, understanding, and sympathizing."

When biologists, zoologists, and agricultural economists cast their eyes on animals, historically, they've focused their attention on the question, "What are you?" The technique for answering that question involves dissection on tables in laboratories. The real question is not "*What* are you?" however. It's "*Who* are you?" Wild horses are individuals. You don't have to observe a mustang for too long before you start to realize there is someone inside that big, magnificent body—someone behind those eyes. As members of their immediate families, larger bonded groups, and extended clans, wild horses know who they are in relation to others. Our challenge is to know that too. We need to understand mustang *biography*, in addition to their biology.

That may require a field or discipline aligned with the humanities, not just the sciences. Our current situation demands a new generation of wild horse philosophers, a group that's big-hearted, open-minded, and sensitive enough to ask moral and aesthetic questions alongside the facts; a group capable of using their narrative imaginations in addition to merely collecting data. There is a precedent. Consider the following excerpt from *The Herring Gull's World* by Niko Tinbergen:

> *It is quite a thrill to discover that the birds you are studying are not simply members of the species Larus argentatus but that they are personal acquaintances. Somehow, the colony becomes much more interesting when you realize that it is composed of individuals that you know personally. Somehow, you feel that you are at home, that you are taking part in their lives, and their adventures become part of your own life. It is difficult to explain this more fully, but I think everyone who has studied animal communities will understand.*

As a way to guard ourselves against sadness in a culture where we exploit animals, we teach each other to dehumanize. Although that practice is understandable, it's also robbed us of an ability to see the similarities and relations between the human and nonhuman. At this stage in our history, however, we stand in need of a discipline that can grapple with all of our relations: our place on the planet and theirs too. We live in a time where we need a field or fields with sincerity enough to allow us to serve as witnesses, an approach humble enough to permit us to become apprentices to the creatures with whom we share so much. In the Bible's book of Job, the advice comes through unmistakably: "Ask the animals and they will teach you."

Again, we have at least the beginnings of a precedent. Barbara Allen recorded the following on a trip to Africa, making observations for an organization called Biosphere. In her book *Animals in Religion: Devotion, Symbol, and Ritual*, she writes:

> *I spent many hours sitting at waterholes. Animals gathered at the water, to partake of that which is essential to life. Some of the animals were bold, others were fearful, but, ultimately, all came to drink; all were refreshed by the same source. Sitting in the hide, compass on my lap, I was awash in a sense of the sacred. The waterhole was a holy space, the compass pointing due north to the sacred. In front of me, and in the shadows, in the spaces where I could not see them but I knew they were there … I experienced, in Lakota terms, Mitakuye Oyasin (All my relations/All are related). I was involved in worship, for, in the words of Simone Weil, 'absolutely unmixed attention is prayer.' Were not my nonhuman brethren also involved in a form of prayer? Were they not totally focused on the ritual, partaking in and of the*

sacramental and the real, the life-giving water? Animals had raised my sacramental consciousness.

In addition to a new generation of wild horse philosophers, I think we're also going to need a group of mustang theologians.

On the side of the road, four of us try to make pictures of a mare grooming a foal. She showers attention on the colt by nipping at his mane. Horses are unlike bison. Technically, they are both prey animals, but bison stand and fight when faced with danger. They swing their skulls and horns to ward off an attack, and thus, the tendency to stand still in the presence of photographers. On the other hand, a horse's only defense is to run. Unlike the other ungulates in North America, horses do not possess any cranial ornaments—no horns, antlers, or paddles protruding out of their skulls. When it comes down to fight or flight, horses were made to flee. When you approach a band of mustangs, there's an ever-present question, "Will they run away?" Anyone who hopes to walk toward a group of wild horses feels the tension. Will they stay? Or will they go?

I am contemplating these questions as I focus my lens. I'm changing aperture settings and shutter speeds. I am not paying attention to the other photographers. Making images of horses is a dynamic undertaking, though. Sooner or later, wild mustangs shift off to another patch of grass or to other interests. After a moment, the horses I'm watching decide to move on, and when they do, I look up and turn to the person next to me. It's a woman, and I can tell she's been crying.

People are the only animals that cry. Of course, we do so for obvious reasons: joy and sadness. In both cases, we leak from our eyes when we feel overwhelmed. There are more nuanced occasions when people weep, however. I have noticed, when people see free-roaming bands of wild horses for the first time, the sight often leads to tears.

On one of our early visits to the Black Hills Wild Horse Sanctuary in South Dakota, Lynn and I took a tour with a guide. We rode in a truck across the property, to a place where mustangs often meet. The drive took half an hour, but we found horses in the spot where we hoped to find them. When we climbed from the truck, I noticed Lynn dabbing her eyes with the cloth we use to clean our cameras.

I asked our guide, "Is that common? Do people cry when they come upon a group of mustangs?"

He said, "Absolutely. Yeah. It happens all the time."

I have seen a good deal of evidence, in the past several years, to suggest that he is right. Lynn and I often drive people out to see wild horses. Misty eyes and tears are typical. It's joy. At least, that's a part of the explanation. My sense is that it's more than happiness, though. Maybe it's something different. When people cry in the presence of mustangs, it's like the outpouring of emotion that we feel in a gallery when we come upon a work of art that touches something in our scaffolding of memories. It's comparable to times when unexpected songs come on the radio, and we find ourselves moved by the feelings that flow from the lyrics or melody. It's happiness, of course. It's sadness too, alongside hope, poignancy, and an element of reverence.

When people see wild mustangs for the first time, they are often struck by the affection the horses display toward each other. In the West, mustangs have hundreds of thousands of acres they can roam as individuals, but they stand with their faces together, squinting into one another's eyes. Of course, they're larger and more physically impressive than us, but they're also better at maintaining families. I think, for many people, when they see a band of wild horses for the first time, it feels like a vision of how mammals ought to relate to each other.

My family is spread out across the continent. We're all successful to some degree. But we've made careers, and real estate, and SUVs, and high technology the focus of our lives. In fact, the more that we succeed, the further we fling ourselves into directions we're supposed to value in our culture: beach resorts, second homes, and ski vacations, for example. The sight of wild horses lazily caring for each other in the sun shocks many of us as an image of what our lives ought to look like. It's a bit like peering into Eden. Calm. Affectionate. In contrast, most of our days are defined by a lack of serenity and the absence of touch.

My take is that people cry in the presence of wild horses because we are so similar. But we're so different. When we watch bands of mustangs, it's like looking into a mirror—with one exception— we do not see a reflection of ourselves. Instead, we see what our society has done to us.

I nod to the woman standing next to me with water in her eyes. I give her a knowing glance. Then I smile with the intent to convey, "I know. Me too."

⁂

It's our last day in the park, so we drive slow through the rest of the circle tour. We stop to look at another colony of prairie dogs. A stand of cottonwoods suggests itself as a spot for a picnic, so we hike into the grove. While we are nestled in the trees, a group of prong-horn wanders by at a distance shorter than usual. We eat sandwiches, drink sparkling water, and talk about the horses that we saw. After a meal in the shade, we decide to finish the drive and head to camp.

On the last stretch of the tour, I notice a silver horse, standing by himself near the top of a ridge. When I flipped through the guidebook to the wild horses in the park, the stallion named Arrowhead captured my attention. The horse ahead of us on the road has a coat that matches the silver tone of the animal that struck me in the gift shop. I nudge Lynn and tell her, "Look. It's Arrowhead." She catches a glimpse of the animal, but she only sees his hindquarters. As we approach, he slips over the horizon.

When we arrive at the top of the hill, we pull off the pavement to see if we can find him. We look along the length of the ridge, but he is gone. I notice a trail made by hooves leading down around a bend, so we start to follow the path. Eventually, the trail shifts to the north and leads us to another view. When we make it past the turn, we find the horse, along with a faraway look out into the landscape.

He appears thinner than the beast that struck me in the guidebook to the park. If this is Arrowhead—the band stallion—it is an older and more solitary version. He looks over his shoulder to examine us. He doesn't leave. At least, not immediately. The animal takes a moment to think about who we are and what we represent. Then he turns and continues down the path in the unhurried way of old people who reach a phase where they become unflappable. Lynn and I exchange a glance, confirming that we shouldn't follow him. We just stand and watch him go.

With the mustang out of sight, we turn our thoughts toward the land. The view from the horse path is better than the one on the circle tour. From our vantage point, we see farther than we could see from the road. The view is stunning, but it is marred by the sight of oil derricks and machinery. In the first decade of the 2000s, the state of North Dakota underwent a boom in energy development. The rigs are not in the park, but they were put in place along its boundary. Rapid drilling gave the region a temporary economic boost, but it's easy to imagine how Theodore Roosevelt would have fought the placement of industrial equipment on the border of the park that bears his name.

As a native of New York, Roosevelt came of age in the city. His family earned a fortune operating factories. He understood the value of commercial endeavors. Roosevelt even made attempts to profit by running a western ranch, but he also understood the thoughtless nature of our lust for capital. His time in the Badlands turned him into a prophet … shaman … seer … sage. His journeys on the borderland between our culture and the wild places left in America gave him insights that most of us never take the time to cultivate. He looked past his own self-interest, and he saw through the mist of immediate personal wishes that, too often, block our ability to make judgments. He looked into the future and saw our broader needs. In an essay from *A Book-Lover's Holidays in the Open*, he makes it plain: "Our duty to the whole bids us to restrain an unprincipled present-day minority from wasting the heritage of unborn generations."

Roosevelt forged his character in the otherworldly landscapes of the West. Of course, one could argue that his character was more than his alone. Some might suggest, as a people, we cut the shape of the American character out on the edges—in the frontier—where wildness and civilization buffed each other to a chrome-like sheen. Roosevelt believed that our spirits are best renewed in nature. In his mind, that made wild places and wildlife worthy of protection. At times, we've taken up conservation with zeal, but the fervor behind our efforts has been waning. We've begun a practice of shrinking the monuments that we established to guard the scenic wonders of the continent. We refuse to protect threatened species on the outside chance that doing so might limit the activities of multinational corporations. Our own government agents remove wild horses from public land, and then they wink when private parties ship them to slaughter in Mexico.

In a 1967 essay for the journal *Science*, the historian Lynn White suggested, "What people do about ecology depends on what they believe about who they are." Who are we, in the end? There were times when, as a nation, we could have considered ourselves the heirs of Theodore Roosevelt. Today, a claim like that would feel strained or even false. We let our culture back us into a corner—with careers on our minds, phones in our hands, and a range of obligations spread out before us. When we came to think of ourselves primarily as workers, we grew intent on consumption. After that, it became hard to hold any space open for adventure or time spent in contemplation. When you're embedded in a way of life, it becomes hard to imagine another type of existence. Even so, I am not telling any secrets by suggesting there's a growing sense that, when it comes to the character of our daily lives, and perhaps the course of the nation, something is going wrong. But questions dog us at this juncture. What will we do?

Throughout the previous 30,000 years of human history, we would have likely turned to a shaman in times like these—a person with wisdom and an ability to stand outside the norms and values that govern the actions of the group. We don't turn to shamans anymore. Even if we did, I'm not sure where we'd look. Still, as I watch the campfire on our last night in the park, it occurs to me that Theodore Roosevelt's example may have little to do with the importance of sages or shamans or critics or leaders. With my eyes stuck to the flames twirling upward along the bank of the Little Missouri, I am reminded that Roosevelt turned to no one for assistance. At watershed moments in his biography, he looked to wild country. Time and solitude were the tools he used to re-story his life. He took to the wilderness as a way to refashion himself as a new kind of person.

It is quiet by the fireside. Lynn and I are both reflecting on the day. When it's time to start thinking about going to bed, she stands and makes her way toward the teepee.

From inside, I hear her ask, "Do you think that silver horse was Arrowhead?"

I don't even have to think. I say, "Yeah. He's just a little older now."

At least, that's the memory I am taking with me from the trip. When it comes to memories, and the life stories that they stack up to form—we write and curate them ourselves. On our last night in the park, that thought gives me a measure of comfort. I take one last sip of wine from my Roosevelt souvenir mug. Then I toss the little bit that's left onto the campfire. The flame shudders, but then it begins coming back. The fire continues to burn.

ENCHANTED BY A GHOST TOWN

I think I could turn and live with animals, they are so
placid and self-contain'd,
I stand and look at them long and long.
They do not sweat and whine about their condition,
They do not lie awake in the dark and weep for their sins ...
Not one is dissatisfied, not one is demented with the mania of
owning things

—Walt Whitman, *Song of Myself*

Most of the wild horses in Wyoming live in a dry expanse that we loosely describe as the Red Desert. There are mountains in this desert, however, and they are green. In Arizona and the Southwest, they call peaks that rise from arid basins "sky islands." Out to the left of the Mississippi, if the terrain tilts above 7,000 feet, you can expect to find an alpine or subalpine ecosystem. Seen from low altitude, a tree-covered mountain takes on the appearance of an island or oasis.

Mountains enjoy a high level of popularity. They capture our thoughts as ideal sites for recreation. We hike their slopes and ski down them in the winter. We pitch our tents in the shade of the conifers, and we make photos of mountain peaks. This approach to high country is fairly new, however. Throughout most of our history, we saw mountains as places to avoid. We pictured them as difficult. We dreaded the weather and steep pitches. We feared the gnarled crags that separated us from our destinations. As the history of the West unfolded, settlers spent time looking for passes or routes that kept them from having to cross over mountain ranges.

The psychologist James Hillman spent a good part of his career researching the relationship between our vision and our habitat. He drew a conclusion: "We see what our ideas let us see." In 1970, Walter Hickel, then governor of Alaska, gave a speech on the subject. With regard to the Alaskan landscape, he said, "Two years ago it was the hostile frozen North, now all of a sudden it's the goddamn delicate tundra." In the same year, 1970, we celebrated Earth Day for the first time as a nation. During all of our history prior, our culture kept us from seeing the earth as something we might celebrate.

Hikers, campers, and wild horse enthusiasts have an easy time accessing the forests of the sky islands on the north side of the Red Desert. A gravel road leads to the top of Green Mountain, for example. In a passenger car, it's possible to drive above 8,000 feet. We didn't build the roads for fly fishers, mountain bikers, or mustang seekers, however. Generally, when we use tax dollars to scrape roads onto rural landscapes, we do it for trucks that carry logging, mining, and oil drilling equipment.

In spite of attempts to put "America first" in our system of values, it is foreign-based companies that run the mines and oil fields on public land—your land and my land—in the West. In the northern part of the Red Desert, a South African mining conglomerate, Rio Tinto, owns the largest operation. Elsewhere in the region, it's corporations like Royal Dutch Shell, British Petroleum, and the Canadian energy giant, Encana, that manage the digging and drilling enterprises. We make it easy for them. We sell foreign companies the right to drill our property. Then we tax American families and use the funds that we collect to build roads for the South African, Canadian, and European prospectors. The roads lead right to the places where they claim and then extract our resources.

The practice occurs so often, and in so many US states, the Forest Service maintains more miles of roadway than the Federal Highway Administration. By far, the bulk of the roads were put in place to serve the interests of multinational companies, although I travel them myself, searching for wild horses or just a good spot to watch the sunset. I've been carried to scenic views in the process, but I've also found the industrial wreckage of abandoned mines and drilling sites. Foreign companies often fold up the division that drills in the United States when the oil or minerals run out. That makes it possible to leave rotting equipment where it lies, without having to pay to clean it up. Businesspeople treat a well-timed bankruptcy as standard operating procedure.

In a book called *The Old Ways*, the anthropologist Wade Davis takes time to think about our willingness to offer up our riches, and our curious inclination to live with the consequence, after corporations from other countries take what they want from our landscape. He writes, "Think for a moment about what these practices say about our society. We accept as normal that people who have never visited our land—people with no history or connection to our country—may come in and transform or even desecrate our place."

Native Americans have been known to describe white people as "moon children." One Navajo woman put it this way: "They must have come from the moon, 'cuz they have no respect for the Earth, and they're so pale."

Personally, I repurpose the network of roads on our prairies and mountains to good effect. Logging roads have carried me to streams where I've caught trout. I've dodged oil truck traffic on my way to look for campsites, and I've used our web of roads to stage trips to some of the highest peaks in Wyoming and Utah. The roads are not ideal when you're attempting to find horses, however. They were built to carry logging and drilling equipment, but mustangs rarely live in the places that harbor the goods that appeal to mining or timber companies. On Green Mountain, for example, a graded gravel road winds along a creek and through a forest to the top, but horses rarely spend time in the woods.

The road to the top of Green Mountain does not meander through horse habitat, but it does provide a series of scenic lookout points for motorists. In one case, drivers see a view to the west that opens up enough to encompass an entire watershed. If you stop to look, you can see a valley, with Sheep Creek churning at the bottom. You can also see the slope that rises on the other side of the stream. From the road, you have to look through the trees to see into the distance, but on the far side, there is no forest. It's a meadow.

Early settlers called the area Sheep Park. In the past, sheep herders occupied the knoll in the summer. Today, it's cattle ranchers that run their stock up to the park to eat the grass. With binoculars, you're likely to see cows in the clearing, but I have also seen mustangs. Unfortunately for me, stockmen ride all-terrain vehicles, so the government did not feel pressed to build a fully graded road into Sheep Park.

I do not own an ATV, so for several years I dismissed Sheep Park as a place I'd never see in person. Then my local sporting goods store started to carry canvas bags that fit on racks attached to mountain bikes. There are few places on a mountain that I cannot reach on a bicycle. So last summer I made a plan. With my camera and lens tucked in a pack, along with two full meals, rain gear, and enough water for a couple of days if necessary, I set out for Sheep Park.

I leave Casper before sunrise with my bike clamped to the roof of our car. I drink coffee on the highway to Jeffrey City, the closest place to the spot where you make the turn to Green Mountain. To avoid having to fit a third meal in a canvas bag, I plan to eat breakfast at the Split Rock Bar, the only restaurant for more than fifty miles.

Jeffrey City is no city. It's not even a village. It's a ghost town. In 1955, geologists found evidence of uranium in the area. At the time, we were building nuclear power plants, and we needed fuel to run them, so we built a mine, and then we built a city for the miners. At the height of the boom in the uranium market, 4,500 people lived outside the open pit at Jeffrey City. Then, in 1981, the market changed. Cheaper ore became available. The main operation closed—so did the general store, gas stations, hotel, swimming pool, apartments, two out of three churches, and all but one of the taverns. Today, from what I can tell, about two dozen people live in the area full-time. They live in the ruins of a formerly fire-preaching, whiskey drinkin', mining town.

If you pay attention in the West, it becomes clear that corporations leave more than just industrial wreckage on the landscape. They also leave cultural rubble. Western communities rarely form around ties to a place or its people. Instead, they spring up next to capital investments. Cities form around financial speculations. Then when the speculations change, dreams are dashed, families are cracked apart, and one-time towns are left to turn into dilapidated monuments to our short-sightedness.

Still, I like eating breakfast at the Split Rock Bar. There are stains on the floor from beer that spilled in the late 1960s and early 1970s, but that's alright. The eggs taste good and the waitress tells exceptional stories. If you catch her on the right morning, she'll talk about the old times and the characters who used to drink their paychecks at the bar. It's a nice meal.

When I'm finished, I head for the parking lot. Outside, on a broken-down and boarded up old store, somebody took the time to paint a sign. On a white background, in upper-case letters, the sign says, "JESUS." When it comes to words, it's the same as we find when we look at a landscape. Our ideas shape what we see. When I first saw the sign, I thought, "Jesus. Yeah. Jesus—what the *hell* happened to *this* town?" Later on, I began to imagine that people passing through the region might interpret the sign with something more like a question mark: "Jesus?" I started to think that visitors might wonder out loud to the Lord about the future of the place.

Now when I look at the sign, set on a street where nearly everyone and everything is gone, it feels like someone put it there to suggest that Jesus still lives in Jeffrey City, even though everybody else packed their clothes into their pickups and drove off. I imagine that notion gives at least a little bit of comfort to those who choose to stay.

⚬▾▴▾⚬▴▾⚬

Driving up the gravel road to Green Mountain, I begin to suspect that the waitress at the Split Rock is the last person I will see for a while, but I don't mind. I grew accustomed to long hours by myself when I was a younger man. In the decade of my twenties, I raced mountain bikes. The only way to succeed in that endeavor is to spend big blocks of time preparing for events. Some of those hours you clock with friends and training partners, but sports like mountain biking also demand long stretches of solitude.

I made good use of my time alone on a bike. As an undergraduate, and later as a graduate student, I had plenty to think about. The time to myself gave me a chance to consider, and then reconsider, all of the things that I am supposed to understand as a sociologist. I worked a lot of things out by myself on the seat of a bicycle. I took up fly fishing for trout later, after I began a career and I could no longer manage a training schedule. Angling and backpacking to remote creeks added up to even more hours alone.

By the end of those trips, I'd look forward to seeing Lynn again and sitting on my couch under my reading lamp. But the trips allowed me to blow the dust out of the space between my synapses. We need time alone to form our own thoughts, and to forge our own connections between ideas. Solitude and uninterrupted time allow us the only way to begin to think independently. In our era, however, solitude is growing difficult to find. The philosopher Søren

Kierkegaard, who never even lived to see a computer or a cell phone, had this to say in his book *Works of Love*: "It is a frightful satire and an epigram on the modern age … that the only use for solitude is to make it a punishment, a jail sentence." We grow up thinking of "time out" as a reprimand.

Between 2010 and 2013, a team of researchers from Harvard and the University of Virginia conducted a series of eleven studies on solitude. They placed subjects in an unadorned room, by themselves, for a period of between six and fifteen minutes. No cell phones. They asked the participants to spend their time "thinking." They only gave people one option outside of being alone with their thoughts. As a substitute for sitting and thinking, they were permitted to shock themselves with a painful jolt of electricity. Two-thirds of the men and a quarter of the women in the study pushed the shock button as an alternative to simply sitting by themselves with just the company of their own thoughts.

Near the top of Green Mountain, I have a chance to use binoculars to scout the situation in Sheep Park. The sun's rays are horizontal and the light is dim, so I squint across the valley between the road I'm driving and the meadow on the other side of the divide. My binoculars jump my vision over the distance. That allows me to look into the setting.

We're a nation of screen watchers. We spend most of our days staring at monitors, either on desktops or in hand. As a result, our world has largely become two-dimensional. Our daily routines don't afford us much of a chance to practice looking into the distance. More than ever, we spend our time "looking at" flat surfaces, as opposed to "looking into" our surroundings. It seems we traded depth for the smooth glass on our devices.

Even through binoculars, I cannot see any mustangs. Sheep Park looks empty but I'm not deterred. I wrestle my bike from the rack on the roof of the car, and then I load my gear. After a week spent poring over maps, I concluded it is possible to travel down a two-track to the west, along the south side of the mountain. By the look of things, the westerly route will skirt me around the canyon carved by Sheep Creek. Once I'm on the other side, I concede that I will need to find a route, but the topo lines on the map make it seem like I should be able to ride back to the north and into the grass of Sheep Park.

Years of erosion cut deep ruts into the Jeep path at the top of Green Mountain. It takes a certain amount of route finding just to keep my two wheels on the road. I manage to navigate the first three miles without incident, but then the path starts to become defined by unrideable hills and harrowing descents. I walk the bike when the terrain tilts up too high. On the downsides of the hills, I ride. Loose gravel on the trail makes it difficult to steer, but I hold my course— right up until I don't.

I am going too fast. I start to lose traction, and the bike comes out from under me. My hip and elbow dig into the gravel. The crash tears the bag on my left side off of its rack, squashing my sandwiches, bananas, and corn chips. I keep my face off of the ground, however. I consider that good luck. My camera and lens also appear safe. Before I climbed onto the bike, I moved them into my backpack.

On the side of the road, I take a minute to assess my scrapes. Then I take another moment to swear and utter curse words at the universe. "God damn it!" "What the hell!?" The bicycle I am riding came with a sticker on the frame: "Adventure by bike." I ordinarily remove logos and decals from my bicycles, but this one stayed. In English, the word "travel" has roots in an older term, one that's still in our vocabulary: "travail." Despite the cuts, bruises, and cursing, I believe, like the makers of my mountain bike, a good journey presents you with a struggle.

⁂

From a high point on the west side of the mountain, I can see that I have made it past Sheep Creek and its canyon. I am now parallel with the park and ready to descend into the meadow. I assumed that I would need to find my own route, but I find a game trail instead. A combination of elk, horse, and cow hoofprints lead me down through the forest. Once I make it out of the trees and onto the prairie, the trail grows too dispersed to follow. There are no roads through Sheep Park. Even so, the tires on my bike glide over the top of the grasses.

Until this moment, I had only ever seen the park from a mountain away. From a distance, I couldn't see the degree to which the landscape undulates—it heaves and surges. I stop while I am still on the south end of the meadow. I cannot see across. I only see the stretch of prairie fifty yards in front of me, rising up to a ridge that's tall enough to block the view. My curiosity propels me to the top, and when my eyes come over the crest of the prairie-wave, I see two dozen elk. They're laying down. Fortunately, I hit my brakes before my bike and body become visible.

I pull my camera from its case. Then, on my knees, I slink up through the vegetation. The plants are knee-high in Sheep Park, so I find enough cover to keep myself hidden. Most of the elk are nestled on the ground. At the edge of the group, however, two bulls stand together, snacking on forage. I am struck by the size of them. The largest outweighs me by 500 pounds, or maybe more. St. Peter said, "All flesh is grass." The big elk give me an occasion to think about the sprouts pressing through the soil underneath my hands and knees. I manage to make a series of images without upsetting the herd. Then I back my bike away from the top of the ridge.

Now my only option in the search for horses is to travel north across the prairie. With no trail in front of me, I enjoy a sense of freedom that's rarely possible in our culture. I roll where my wishes take me, and I make good time crossing the park, but I don't find any horses.

A lone tree stands at the north end of the meadow, so I decide to make the shade it offers the site of a meal. Over time, it appears that horses used the tree to rub their manes and scratch their itches. In so doing, they stamped a ring of flattened dirt and rock around its base. It's a perfectly level place to set a stove. After ten minutes, I am eating ramen noodles in the shade of a ponderosa pine. From Sheep Park, I can see down the mountain onto the sage flats that surround Jeffrey City. The calm air warrants my attention. In Wyoming, it is a rare moment when the wind isn't buffeting your ears. In between bites, I am reminded of a book called *The Roads Have Come to an End Now* by the Norwegian poet Rolf Jacobsen. He understood, in our city lives, we need to search for quiet, "*The silence that lives in the grass / on the underside of each blade / and in the blue space between stones.*"

The shriek of a stallion interrupts my musings. It's one of nature's most unmistakable sounds—a wild horse's voice at high volume. From my perch under the pine, I can tell the noise came from behind me to the south. I don't have to look hard to find the source, however. It's a band of six mustangs I recognize. Closest to me, it's a stallion that Lynn and I call "Tuffy." Apparently, when I heard the commotion, he had been having words with his lead mare, Jigsaw, known for her painted coat, reminiscent of puzzle pieces set across her sides.

Bird-watchers tell stories about what they call their "spark birds." That is, the species or sighting—the experience—that turned them into birders. In nearly every case, a bird-watcher can tell you the species that inspired them to spend more than they should on field guides and vacations to well-known birding spots. I've heard more than one person cite the blue heron as their source of inspiration. In my case, it was the pelican. I came to know them years ago, while spending time on rivers, fly fishing for trout. Then I started to look for them in the sky. They soar at such high elevation that they often appear as tiny pale dots in the atmosphere. That sparked my need for a decent pair of binoculars.

My spark horse was Ponyboy, the lonely bachelor stallion. We looked for him often, but we only saw Pony a few times over a course of months. In contrast, I've seen Tuffy off and on for seven years, and it's the hope of spotting him that keeps me coming back to Green Mountain. He's a small pinto with black and white patches on his body. He only stands fourteen hands tall, but I've seen him take on rival stallions two hands taller, maybe more. Tuffy's the boss. He knows that, and the other horses seem to know it too. He doesn't have to prove himself, and that level of certainty gives him an easy demeanor. Tuffy is not afraid of other horses, and he's never been afraid of me. That has meant that I've been able to make close-up pictures of him.

With my camera at my side, I walk out from under the tree and onto the prairie toward Tuffy. The composition of a stallion's band is subject to change, but today he shares the company of three mares and two foals. Two of the mares have been with Tuffy for the whole time that I've known him. My initial movement catches their attention, but I have spent hours with this band, and horses possess memories that match or exceed ours. They recognize me. After a moment, their thoughts turn back to each other and to eating.

I usually avoid making images of horses while they're eating. They eat a lot. You often find them with their heads bent to the ground, but I prefer to wait until I can see their faces. Eventually, grazing horses look up to scout for trouble or a new enticing bed of greenery, but in the case of this band, it takes a while to find a moment when one of them rises from their food.

I position myself closest to Tuffy. I'm hoping to make an image of his face and mane. He has "curly" in his family tree. In the past, curly horses were found in the herds bred by the Choctaw tribe. It's clear at least some of Tuffy's ancestors were of Choctaw descent. His white mane falls on his neck in a crimped-up, sort of corkscrew wave. It's a visual complement to his painted neck and chest.

Slowly, I try to move in closer, but every time I take two steps, he matches my distance by moving further in the same direction. He doesn't even lift his head. After several attempts to close the gap between us, I sit down. "Patience," I tell myself. I take a seat on the prairie and wait.

While I sit in the grass, a red-tailed hawk makes circles in the sky above. I train my lens on the bird of prey. As the raptor swings in looping arches in the air, I do my best to time my exposures around the sun illuminating her feathers. I lay on my back to track her flight.

While I am stationary and preoccupied, Tuffy grazes his way toward me. By the time I sit up to find him again, he stands twenty feet away and he is not eating. He's staring at my face. He has a mouthful of grass, but he is not chewing. He's just staring at me.

People who spend time with horses often describe scenarios where the animals "look right through them," to the point where it feels like they're "reading your mind." It's a common impression, and it is common for a reason—horses *can* read minds.

In the early part of the twentieth century, a man named Wilhelm von Osten made a living as the proprietor of "Clever Hans," a horse with a knack for mathematics. In cities all over Germany, before stadiums full of spectators, von Osten presented Hans with math problems printed on poster-sized paper. In response, Hans tapped his answers on the ground with his front hooves. During the course of the show, the problems became more sophisticated. That didn't seem to matter, though. The horse still answered correctly.

Even so, skeptics questioned the animal's skills. They increased the difficulty of the problems. Zoologists presented Hans with even tougher questions, but that didn't stump him. They found the horse equal to the challenge. Finally, as a way to test Hans in a laboratory-like setting, they asked him a series of questions in an environment where he was on his own in a stall, without the presence of von Osten or any other observers. They found, with no one else around, the horse's ability faded. Without onlookers he couldn't add or subtract.

Commentators on the study concluded that Hans never calculated his answers to math problems. Instead, he read the bodies and expressions of the people in the room. When he tapped his hoof on the ground, he watched their anticipation rise. When he had reached the right number of taps, he could also see that in the faces of those watching him. He read the thoughts of the people in his environment for years without a flaw. Some people were disappointed that Hans was not making calculations, but he was actually doing something even more impressive.

It turns out that horses think differently than us. As human beings, we tend to want to shrink the rich world of the present moment down into digits. Horses have no reason to do that, so they don't, but having evolved as prey on the grasslands of prehistoric North America, they have good reason to read the minds of other animals, including ours.

Tuffy understands me. I've never been able to hide anything from this horse. He knows I am here to see him, so he grudgingly abides by letting me make a photo of his face. Then he returns to eating grass.

⁂

The afternoon begins to melt away. The foals lay down with their mothers looming above them. Tuffy takes a post forty feet from his band, on a low rise. Then he shuts his eyelids. I set my camera down and take time to read from a book of poems by Jim Harrison.

Eventually, the calm in the meadow is broken by the presence of another band. A bay stallion, two mares, and a foal wander into the park. The stallion is massive. In the past, regiments of the United States cavalry let some of their draft horses loose when tactics changed and they were ordered to leave a fort. From there, the great animals fell in with bands of mustangs. Today, most of the wild horses in Wyoming conform to the size and traits preferred by Spanish explorers and Native American tribes, but some of them are large and forcefully muscled. Their ancestors spent their days drawing metal plows across unbroken soil.

Tuffy sees them first. He shakes me from my book with a grunt-like whinny. Then, when I look up, he's tossing his head in the air as a signal to the bay stallion: "You're in my territory." It's too late, however. The bay stallion has changed his course and he is coming over.

As I put my book down and pick up my camera, Tuffy makes a move. He's headed for a confrontation. Both horses pick up speed. It only takes a moment for the animals to meet, and when they do, the bay stallion rears up on his hind legs. Tuffy rises too. At the top of the motion, he lashes at the larger horse's throat. Then they fall together. With their hooves back on the ground, they arch their necks and put their faces together. Both horses snort through their noses. Tuffy pounds a hoof in the dirt, causing dust to billow up between them. Then he shrieks into the ear of his opponent. The strategy seems to work. The dust and noise appear to suffice as a deterrent. I am releasing my shutter at times that feel right, but I don't know. I cannot think—it's a storm of equine muscle and testosterone. It feels like I am caught in the throes of the conflict. When the bay stallion walks back to his band and nudges them toward the south, I'm struck by a sense of relief.

In an essay for *Parabola* subtitled "The Long, Pure Look," Padma Hejmadi describes the impact of making photographs at times when the subject is engrossing. Early in the work, she offers an analysis of the term "dhyana," a concept that appears in ancient Sanskrit. The word translates as both "attention" and "meditation," with connotations that suggest an "illuminated moment" or an instance where the "spirit is stretched." Hejmadi explains what can occur behind the lens of a camera:

> *At some point, you are seeing so intensely that you become what you see, you merge ... until the 'you' disappears. The how and whys and wherefores disappear too. Yet when you emerge, you are somehow replenished.*

A growing body of research suggests that equine therapy—time spent with horses—proves effective as a treatment for a range of the afflictions that we suffer from. Evidence supports the claim that the technique diminishes the effects of depression, anxiety, and post-traumatic stress. Studies support the idea that horse therapy works, but scientists encounter trouble when it comes to explaining "how" the method works, or "why?"

That is in part because we expect scientists to use the tools of science. That limits what we can look for and what we can find. Over the course of human history, the use of the scientific method has led to uncanny discoveries and innovations. But in pursuit of an answer to a big question, the insistence on the techniques of science can become a liability. For example, spending time in the presence of animals that are larger and more elegant than we are makes us feel good; we have the data to show that, but charts and graphs cannot provide a good explanation as to how it works or why it's true.

In contrast, most of our wisdom traditions contain messages about the value of appreciating something larger than oneself. It's a deity in the case of Christianity and Islam, and something as simple as service to humankind in the case of Buddhism. Despite differences in doctrine, the aims of spirituality, and the religions of the world, are remarkably similar. When we engage in the rituals associated with our belief systems, at some level, they all attempt to shift our thoughts and views away from a common tendency: introspection. They attempt to move our focus outward, out into the world.

Many of the ill-feelings we suffer from grow out of our disposition toward a narrowly focused type of self-analysis. While we're navel-gazing, we see our self-interests and our state, and we place them beside questions about whether we are meeting the expectations embedded in our culture. We spin webs of narrative about who we are in relation to others, for the better and for the worse. In contrast, the sight of a horse redirects our attention. In the case of equine therapy, the touch of a horse demands our absorption even further. In time spent with a beast more than five times bigger than yourself, it's hard to think about anything but them, and it turns out—that's therapeutic.

I always pack a headlamp, so I'm safe to travel in unfamiliar places after dark. Still, my internal clock is nudging me. My day with the wild horses of Sheep Park is coming to an end. I put my camp stove back in its pack and secure the bags onto my bike. I roll past Tuffy and his band at a distance that keeps them comfortable. I trust that I am the first person-on-a-bicycle that they have ever seen. They look at me with a type of curiosity you might see at a carnival side show. I imagine they wonder at the novelty of the machine and me.

Before I leave the park, I take a moment to soak up the scenery. From a tall point on the prairie, I can still see Tuffy's band behind me, to the north. I take a deep, high-diver breath before I leave the grasslands and enter the forest on the trail that leads back to the top of the mountain. In an interview for *Outside* magazine, the bird biologist Bernd Heinrich told the editors, "We all want to be associated with something greater and more beautiful than ourselves, and nature is the ultimate. It is the one thing we can all agree on."

I've taught on college campuses for more than twenty years. In that time, we've watched rates of anxiety and depression rise in the student body. Suicide rates have also been climbing, across all age groups, through the last decade. We hold the world in our hands, on our devices. We can see anything that we can imagine on our screens, but the backlit images are flat. As we increased the amount of time we spend staring at monitors, we began to lose our depth perception—the ability to picture ourselves happy and content.

In *Beauty: The Invisible Embrace,* John O'Donohue paraphrases the seventeenth-century thinker Blaise Pascale by suggesting, "In difficult times you should always carry something beautiful in your mind." The climb back to the top of the mountain is arduous, but my load is lightened by the band of wild horses I carry. They'll go home with me inside my head and in my camera. On the landscape of my thoughts, the events of the day will stay alive and three-dimensional. I expect my recollections of the afternoon on the mountain will help if I ever find myself in a place or time where I would benefit from restoring the memories.

AFTER THE ROUNDUP

The romantic story of the American wild horse is being brought, out of necessity, to an end . . . in strict accord with the practical necessities of range agricultures, the work of ridding the plains of wild horses goes on . . . they eat too much grass.

—Russell Lord, *The Cattleman*

Viewing nature as optional—as always elsewhere or in the past— denies us, or spares us, the work of caring.

—Kyo Maclear, *Birds Art Life*

In the summer of 2018, the Bureau of Land Management hired a helicopter pilot and a crew to round up and remove wild horses from Green Mountain in Wyoming. They did so without me because I do not attend roundups. I am glad that other people are willing to serve as witnesses, but I cannot. I've heard the stories. I have seen the photos and the footage. Lynn makes some of the images and she also records videos. They always strike me as the same. When the Bureau of Land Management sets up a roundup chute, in essence, they are setting up a funnel to drain the wildness and majesty from public land. It's not something I can bear to watch in person.

By the force of law, photographers are made to stand a good distance from the roundup as helicopters drive bands of horses from the range. Some of the animals are run to death before they reach the chute. Those that are captured face unfamiliar confines, and sometimes they meet unsympathetic handlers. Of the horses that arrive at the roundup site, not all of them make it to long-term holding pens alive. They injure themselves or they're injured while being taken into custody. Then they are euthanized. In the presence of an American mustang receiving mistreatment, I'm not sure that I would stay in the "observation spot." I know myself. I'd try to intervene and that would not work out for the horses or me or the BLM agents involved. Still, I am grateful that Lynn and others like her spend entire days watching and filming as chopper pilots chase terrified mustangs into pens that represent an end to their freedom.

Photography is a powerful tool. Today, sophisticated cameras can upload directly to the internet. For generations, people used the phrase, "The whole world is watching," when trying to keep people from doing shameful things. Since no one wants to feel ashamed, cameras hold the potential to encourage good behavior.

Images are also evidence. Mustang advocates use photos and video to document which bands were removed from their homes and then separated. Nonprofit horse sanctuaries often work to re-unite families, and those efforts are aided by having a record of who went where. Plus, people take pictures of the things they care about.

For wild horse enthusiasts, a roundup often marks the last time they will see their favorite band of mustangs.

The BLM staff members who run roundups don't carry cameras. After they're finished for the day, I suspect they would rather forget. For the officials who order and manage the roundup and long-term storage of wild horses, they consider the procedure a part of their job description. From a professional standpoint, they cannot afford to become emotionally invested in the welfare and future of any particular families of mustangs, or even wild animals in general. To succeed as members of a federal bureaucracy, BLM employees carry out orders.

In order to further their careers, the men and women of the Bureau also need to continue their education, and that is where I come in. Over the years, I've had many local and regional BLM employees in my classes. No surprise—at some point in the semester, the conversation turns toward the management of wild horses. As students, BLM employees often good-naturedly needle me by saying things like, "Hanson. You need to understand—horses are livestock. All of the debates and lawsuits and hurt feelings will go away as soon we start to think about them and treat them as livestock." I appreciate the point of view as a protective mechanism against grief. Reducing our view of animals down to where we see them as saleable items makes their management easier, at least from an emotional standpoint.

I grew up in a family that raised, grew, and collected its own food. We hunted and fished. We kept chickens, rabbits, and a small number of cattle to send to market. I know the lessons that go along with buying and selling creatures or harvesting them from their habitat. In order to live with our actions toward them when we treat them as commodities, we need to downgrade animals in our imaginations. For those who grow their own food or produce it for others, a certain kind of hardening has to take place, starting when kids are young. You have to harden yourself against feelings of empathy toward the animals that you will eventually slaughter or put on a truck to a meatpacking facility. The process begins at home on the ranch or farm. It moves through organizations like 4-H, and then it continues in university-based colleges of agriculture.

In the case of the BLM offices that oversee wild horses, each unit attempts to employ at least one "Horse and Burro Specialist." Ironically, those staff members are seldom horse or burro specialists. They rarely earn degrees in equine studies, ecology, or environmental philosophy. Their education is most often in soil science or agricultural economics. I've sat at tables and talked with them. They tend to see their role as that of advocates for stock grazers. They work within the confines of the Wild and Free-Roaming Horses and Burros Act because that is their job, but they see their role in terms of shrinking horse numbers as opposed to growing them.

No one I've met in the BLM has ever attempted to reduce the number of sheep or cattle in a region as a way to make room for more mustangs. In the time since the passing of the 1971 law that protects them, the areas where wild horses are permitted and the official number allowed on our lands have only declined.

Perhaps for historical reasons, none of this should come as a surprise. The United States Department of the Interior created the BLM in 1946, at a time when they chose to merge the General Land Office, charged with selling public land to encourage development, with the Grazing Service, where the customs and traditions promoted agribusiness. In *Fire on the Mountain*, the desert writer Edward Abbey suggested the letters B-L-M might just as well stand for "Bureau of Livestock and Mining."

When I give talks about mustangs, I tend to field a standard set of questions from the audience. One of the most common is, "Why don't we manage horses on the range?" People ask, "Why don't we just dart the mares with a fertility-control serum and limit the number of new foals born in spring?" It's a good question, so I do my best to explain. I say, "Sometimes, and in some places, that is exactly what we do." Then I cite the Pryor Mountain Range in southern Montana and the McCullough Peaks area near Cody, Wyoming as success stories—places where we rarely round up or remove horses. In these two regions, BLM officials and groups of volunteers manage mustang populations through well-established fertility control programs. I sometimes describe the wild horses of the Cerbat Mountains, north of Kingman, Arizona. In that range, mountain lion predation limits the number of foals that make it to adulthood, rendering roundups and long-term holding pens unnecessary. In most parts of the West, however, roundups and removals continue.

I've met with BLM staff in multiple locations in Wyoming and Colorado. In the process, I've urged the Bureau to adopt plans to end the roundup and long-term warehousing of mustangs by darting mares with a fertility-control drug called *porcine zona pellucida,* or PZP. Most of the time, my pleas meet with skepticism. The objections to managing the number of newborn foals often center on logistics. I have heard, "The area's too big. We'd have to find the mares to dart them—they're too hard to find." I have also been told,

"There's too many black horses out there. They look too much alike. It would be hard to keep a record of the ones we darted and the ones we didn't." A thread of truth runs through these arguments. Some of the areas where mustangs live are really huge, and some horses do look a lot alike, but these are not insurmountable obstacles. There is a better explanation for our reluctance to use humane and affordable practices to manage free-roaming bands of mustangs: personal identity.

Most of the BLM staff who work in the Wild Horse and Burro Program do not think of themselves as conservationists. They don't think of wild horses as wildlife, and they do not identify with the advocates who work to protect or increase the number of mustangs on our prairies. They don't think or talk or dress like nature lovers or enthusiasts. I've spent a good deal of time with people employed by the BLM, and I am trained in sociology and anthropology. But you don't need any degrees in social science to come to this conclusion: BLM staff members think and talk and act and dress like ranchers and cowboys.

As a nation, we placed the Bureau of Land Management in an impossible position. As a nod to the public nature of public land, we charged the agency with managing the property that we all share for what we call "multiple use." That's probably appropriate, but any level of openness to multiple use begs for conflict and division. Imagine the quagmire. Which uses? To what degree? Aren't my values as important as theirs?

Every day these questions surface in BLM offices. Historically, the answers have come down on predictable lines. In the mountains, where there's timber and minerals, the decisions favor logging and mining interests. On the prairie, where there's eatable grass, the decisions favor agribusiness. It's not a scheme, however. There is no conspiracy. In prairie regions, the decisions default in favor of ranching interests because the BLM tends to hire staff members from the ranching communities where their offices are located. By statute, those employees cannot hold grazing leases themselves, but it's been well-documented that agency staff often come from families and social networks that graze private herds of cows on public land.

In my interactions with BLM staff over the years, they have been courteous. I've never had a cross word with any of the men or women who work for the Bureau, but it has also been clear in nearly every case, when it comes to the debate over which animals we should allow to forage on our grasslands, they are members of team cow.

A government roundup of wild horses is an agribusiness-like affair. No tie-dyed shirts. No Birkenstocks, and no Volkswagen microbuses parked in the vicinity. It's cowboy hats, stout-heeled boots, and sizable belt buckles. Men and women alike, BLM staff tend to think of themselves as cowboys, and in spite of the evidence suggesting there are better, more humane, sustainable, and cost-effective means to manage wild horses—*cowboys round things up.*

Still, as the public agency charged with managing the property that we hold in common as a people, the BLM has made an unusual set of choices with regard to our priorities: industrial-scale cattle operations are the largest single occupier of our public lands. Across the nation, we allow cows to consume approximately thirty times the food that we allot to mustangs. We allow private herds of livestock to eat far more forage than we reserve for deer and antelope. By the look of things, you would think that the American people value the subsidization of agribusinesses more than hunting, fishing, hiking, camping, or bird and wildlife watching.

I'm not sure that is true. I am not sure that was ever true, but in this age of urbanization and technology, it seems especially untrue. Today, large numbers of us are searching for a way to balance digital advances with something more essential, primitive, and organic. Americans visit zoos more often than we attend professional sporting or athletic events. We long for something outside of our virtual and economic lives. We search for ways to pull ourselves out of our roles at home and work and into something even just a little bit wild.

Here in the twenty-first century, it would appear that we need the chance to see powerful creatures running free more than we need additional red meat. The truth is, after we allow cattle to eat the plants on our public property, they are increasingly shipped to foreign markets like Japan. Maybe that's just as well. Our own Department of Agriculture's dietary guidelines urge us to consume less beef and spend more time engaged in physical activity. I can't think of a better way to exercise than climbing up a mountain in the West, with the thought of seeing a wild mustang as a prize.

A series of nameless two-track roads fan out from the base of Green Mountain. The roads reach out through a row of shallow valleys that wrinkle the prairie in the basin of the Sweetwater River. Over the years, Lynn and I have mapped the most likely places to find mustangs. Two months after the roundup, we planned a day trip to the spots where we came to know six bands of horses.

It's a state highway that leads out to the area. With Green Mountain in sight, I turn left onto a gravel road. We pass through a barbed wire fence that marks the northern border of the range. Starting out on the dirt trail feels like passing through a turnstile. The possibility of horses reroutes the flow of my attention. It feels like water rushing onto what had been a dried-out riverbed. I am no longer just "driving." Now, each passing moment is part of a quest.

We turn the radio off and creep along the road looking for mustangs. The search is fruitless. All of the places where we used to find them are empty. We drive on, stopping intermittently to scan the horizon, but it's bereft. I am reminded of the words of Saint Hilary: "Everything empty is full of the angels of God." Most of the time, I trust the wisdom of the saints. They always seem astute, but this time I sense no angels. This prairie is haunted. It used to smell like electricity—a sweet mix of horses and sage—a sea of life and sensation. Today, it's a hollow reminder of our foibles: bad planning, unseemly choices, and the subjugation of nature.

We drive all the way to the foot of Green Mountain. In a crook of land where the elevation begins to tilt upward, a series of springs creates a row of perennial mud puddles. In dry country, a puddle is a big attraction. During the last six years, we've never been to this spot without seeing horses, at least somewhere in the viewshed. Today, it's cows and calves, up to their ankles in the water. We pull over and stop to scan the area. Not one single mustang in sight. Lynn and I take a seat on the hood of the car, and for a moment, we watch.

Cows are a human creation. We molded them from the wild bovines of North Africa's prehistory. Most of the modern breeds take their shape from a legacy of European efforts at genetic engineering. Through persistent experiments, we altered their size and lowered their intelligence. Some of their instincts still remain. Cattle orient themselves toward the herd as opposed to bands or families, however. They are unlike horses when it comes to their relationships. The social lives of cows are minimal. Each individual is simply a part of the herd, without unique roles or a way to posture themselves in relation to others. Compared to wild horses, cows appear less cognizant. They pay less attention to their surroundings. If that was not enough, they also wear large, yellow, plastic tags stapled into their ears. Each tag bears a number. A cow is a piece of merchandise.

Something in or near the water spooks a calf. She bolts and runs for twenty feet. It's not a graceful exit, but we did not create cattle to run. We built them to stand in place and put on weight. It's not inspiring to watch one of them move.

In the book *Animal Farm*, a classic parody of the hierarchies that form in human groups, George Orwell quipped, "All animals are equal, but some animals are more equal than others." On public land in the West, all animals are equal, but cows are more equal. We shoot, poison, trap, round up, and remove other species to make room for cattle. Stock growers often complain that horses overgraze our land, but thus far in the twenty-first century, just as an example, the state of Wyoming has played host to more than 1.2 million cows every year, and somewhere between 3,000 and 6,000 wild horses. The situation makes a person wonder, which animals consume more of the state's forage?

Ironically, horses and cows rarely compete for food. Cattle do not usually range more than a mile from a water source, whereas horses will roam ten miles from a pond or stream. Horses also graze steeper slopes than cows—and at higher elevation. Cattle are more likely to stay where they can find a drink. They set up residence beside rivers. In the process, they denude the banks of waterways. They remove the shade plants from the shore, which raises the temperature of creeks. They stand in the current and relieve themselves. That causes contamination. The presence of cows on a river can change its nature for the worse. A well-known fisheries biologist, Robert Behnke, once cited commercial livestock grazing on public land as the greatest threat to the health of trout streams in the West.

Horses rarely spend time in riparian areas, and as a result of their biology, mustangs also graze differently than stock. Critics claim that wild horses trim plants too close to the ground. They possess teeth that work together like scissors. Horses shear off grasses a short distance from the dirt. On the other hand, cows use molar-like teeth to grab their food. Their teeth work in the manner of a plier. Cattle may grip grasses a greater distance from the ground, but they are forced to pull them free, dislodging roots in the process. The next time you get a haircut, ask yourself, would you rather have your stylist use scissors or a pair of pliers? Scissor-like teeth leave roots intact, so plants can live to grow another day.

Horses also replenish their own forage. When they eat from a clump of grass, they return the plants' seeds to the soil in the form of manure. Horse apples contain whole seeds—set to grow. In contrast, cattle ruminate their food through four separate stomach compartments. By the time they excrete the seeds of the plants they have eaten, the kernels are often too eroded to reproduce themselves.

⸱⸱⸱▴▾⸱▾⸱▴⸱▾⸱▴⸱⸱⸱

Prior to the removal of wild horses from Green Mountain, the BLM official in charge was quoted as saying, "We're going to round up every horse that we can find." Those words startled one of the volunteers on the project. In fairness, the agent assumed that they would not find all of the horses. The Green Mountain herd management area contains tens of thousands of acres of sage flats and grassland, but it also contains Green Mountain, and a thick forest covers the high country. Horses prefer open spaces, but at times, mostly out of necessity, they wander among the trees. In particular, mustangs climb up into mountains and woodlands to look for water and cool summer temperatures. Underneath the boughs of pines, they're hidden out of sight.

In August 2018, government officials and contracted staff removed more than 1,200 horses from the vicinity of Green Mountain. At the time, BLM data suggested that approximately 300 mustangs should have been left on the range afterward, most likely in the trees. But the BLM has never established a reliable census. In 2013, the National Academy of Sciences commissioned a report on the federal Wild Horse and Burro program, and one of their strongest findings was that our estimates of wild horse populations are unfounded, often inaccurate. At Green Mountain, BLM staff removed all of the horses they could find. That meant they could have left 300 unaccounted for in the high country. Or they might have left thirty. It is also possible that they left three horses hiding in the forest. Nobody knows.

⁂

Spruce and pine coat the north face of Green Mountain. At the top, things change a bit, however. Near the west end of the range, trees give way to a meadow. At 8,000 feet of elevation, a clearing called Sagebrush Park blankets the crest of the mountain. Stock grazers like to run cattle up to the meadows, where the grasses stay green longer in the summer. As luck would have it, the ground water table also rises surprisingly close to the surface. All that's necessary to create a watering hole is to dig through fifteen feet of sand. Water then fills the space to form a permanent pond. It's astounding. In *The Hidden West*, Rob Schultheis describes a similar place as "a sea inside a desert wrapped in a green prairie."

Horses appreciate Sagebrush Park for obvious reasons: food, water, and open vistas. Lynn and I enjoy the park too. We pitch our canvas teepee on the flatness, in the brush. Because, in our culture, we teach ourselves to value beaches, forests, and mountains, prairie landscapes rarely fetch comparable prices on the real estate market. I suspect our appreciation of grasslands runs in the direction of something more primal than strawberry daiquiris on the shore or posh alpine resorts, however. All of our human roots extend back to the continent of Africa—broad savannahs and flowing knee-high grasses bobbing in the breeze. When I stand in the meadow, looking out across the distance, something from our evolution pulls on the memories inside my cells.

We stop the car and walk into the park to look for wild horses. At 8,000 feet, up in the wide-open, the wind blows through you like you are a skeleton. Out of instinct, collars go up and hands shrink into the sleeves of jackets to conserve the little bit of warmth that the wind doesn't sweep away. We don't find horses, but we know how they like to move across the area. A water hole stands at the edge of the prairie. Horses take a drink and then meander into the clearing to rest and snack on the grasses. We find a high point that affords us a view of the pond, the edge of the forest, and a large swath of the meadow. Then we sit. It's time to wait.

I'm dozing off when I hear Lynn whisper, "Okay." It's a band of four mustangs: a pure black stallion, two sorrel mares, and a mocha-colored colt. We watch the lead mare step from the trees with the young one at her side, the others falling in behind her. I am struck by the confidence and rhythm of her gait. In contrast to the awkward jostling of cattle at the base of the mountain, a band of wild horses emerging from a forest looks like a series of carefully designed explosions of molecular energy, contained in perfectly shaped vessels. There is a fluency to the presence of these creatures—every one of their steps, deft and assured.

A gust of wind shoves at me from behind. It gives me a reason to look down at myself—all bundled up. Out of necessity, we keep our bodies separate from the world. We're wrapped in cotton and nylon stitched in the factories of Asia. Wild horses live directly in their habitat. They drink the wind and dig their hooves into the dirt. When I give talks about mustangs, I am often asked, "Don't they need any shelter from winter storms?" "What about bug spray in the springtime?" "What do they do without horseshoes?" All I say in response is, "Not necessary."

The word "wild" descends from a term in old Norse. When an animal or landscape demonstrated a high level of self-possession, the Vikings would describe them as "willed." In other words, their state or actions were their own, unbent and unfazed by the desires or interests of humankind. In modern English, we split the term "willed" up into "wild" for animals and "wilderness" for places, but the connotation stayed the same.

.⁘▾▴⁘⁖ ▴▾.⁘.

The horses we're watching begin to move down the tree line on their way to the water hole. Before too long, the lead mare takes notice of us. She pauses and turns to the second mare, as if to question her about the level of threat posed by the humans on the hill. The second mare takes a moment to look in our direction. The stallion stops ten feet behind. In a family of horses, the lead mare makes the majority of the decisions. Stallions win their place in a band by performing feats of strength. They maintain their status by facing and fighting off challengers. In contrast, the lead mare in a band of horses is elected. Lead mares negotiate their position by demonstrating care and good judgment. They have to build trust. Friendships. Coalitions.

After a lengthy study of the means that horses use to communicate, in 2015, researchers at the University of Sussex published a report in the peer-reviewed journal *Plos One* describing the equine language of facial expression. Their work resulted in the unveiling of a new system of analysis: EquiFACS—The Equine Facial Action Coding System. Originally meant to identify nonverbal cues and emotions in humans, the system has been applied to a range of other species, most profitably in horses. The Sussex team identified seventeen facial postures and movements that correspond to social contexts and emotional states in the equine world: fear, anger, surprise, and affection, among others. By comparison, orangutans make use of fifteen expressions and chimpanzees limit their nonverbals to thirteen different gestures. The only two species that communicate with more complex systems than horses are cats at twenty-one, and human beings with a total of twenty-seven discernible signals.

We share a lot with horses. They have large, sophisticated brains, and they lead complex social lives. As an observer of mustangs, it's easy to see how their actions mimic ours. That makes it tempting to want to describe equine behavior by drawing correlations to our own thoughts and actions. All we can do is try to put ourselves in their place. When we do, we begin to imagine what it would be like to be a horse. It is by imagining ourselves in their minds, and looking out through their two eyes, that we attempt to interpret the gestures that they make toward each other. I find myself thinking like this: "If I was a wild stallion taking time to nuzzle my lead mare, what would I be saying to her?"

Sociologists call this "role taking." We do it all the time. By imagining ourselves in another person's position, we can, with some degree of accuracy, know what it's like to be them. It's a common and healthy part of human life. When we spend time with others, we start to empathize. We begin to put ourselves in people's shoes. When we spend time with animals, we do the same thing. We start to try to imagine what it might be like to be them.

We do it with dogs and cats. When my cat Sherpa meows in the morning after she's eaten, I try to put myself in her place and ask, "What is she saying?" We've done this with gorillas and chimpanzees and dolphins, and some of us do the same thing with wild horses. Role taking allows us to imagine what it would be like to be a horse. That's fun to think about, of course, but the real question is, "What is it like for a *horse* to be a horse?" And that's harder to know. It's one of the reasons that I don't attend roundups—too much wondering and questions that we can't answer. What does it feel like for a family of mustangs to have a helicopter descend on them from the sky? What are the captured mares saying when they scream as their young are taken from them and placed into holding pens?

⁙▾▿⁙▴▾⁙

Through the lens of my camera, I watch the family of horses we've been studying take their last steps toward the water hole. The lead mare looks at us, and then she bends her head to drink. It makes me wonder about the horses that we drove from here with a helicopter. It's impossible to know exactly where they are today. They're likely standing in feedlots in as many as three different US states. Do they look out through the bars of their holding pens and think of Green Mountain? What do they picture as a memory? I wonder if Sagebrush Park lives in their minds as a holy place.

Several lines of research, and practical experience, have established that horses possess effective long-term memories. For reasons of survival, they compose detailed and lasting cognitive maps of their surroundings. They build working mental pictures of food sources, water, threats, and topography. We give a standard piece of advice to new sheep herders in Wyoming. We say, "If the snow starts coming down too hard and you can't see—if you get lost—take the bridle off your horse's head, hang on, and stay quiet. She knows where she is. Let her take you back to camp."

After they drink, the horses wander onto the prairie. The foal grooms her mother's neck with carefully placed bites along the length of her mane. The stallion closes his eyes and kinks a back leg in—the sign that he has gone to sleep. Lynn and I walk over to the car. We store our cameras in the backseat. Then I hear Lynn say, "Come on."

We're only parked thirty yards from the edge of the mountain. On its south side, Sagebrush Park drops off to the expanse of the Red Desert, 2,000 feet below. Lynn starts walking toward the edge and I follow. When we arrive at a ledge with a view to the south, we stop without having to say a word. We take seats on boulders and stare out into the distance. The psychologist Bernard Aaronson once had this to say about the type of precipice we're on:

> *The traditional association of mountaintops with the abode of deities may be less because they are higher than the areas around them than because they make possible those experiences of expanded depth, in which the self can invest itself in the world and expand across valleys.*

I'm not sure what's better, our height in relation to the desert below, or the desert below, but either way, I believe Aaronson is onto something. This is not the first time I've felt part of me expanding into a long view.

There is an old Hindu proverb that states, "The soul that beholds beauty becomes beautiful." I look at Lynn. She's been good for my soul for a quarter of a century. I'm often surprised at how we find ourselves alone in places like these, however. We're not that far from home. Aside from some occasional hunters in the fall, and a handful of families on all-terrain vehicles in the summertime, we rarely meet anyone on top of the mountain. I am afraid, for those of us who live beside the wild, rolling plains, free-roaming bands of mustangs are a little like the stars. We can see them almost any night, so we almost never take the time.

It makes me wonder, what will future generations say about us? Will they think of us as wise? Will they see us as fools? When they think of us, will they say, "Here is a generation that loved beauty?" Will they take pride in our efforts to protect a modicum of wildness in an otherwise domesticated and commercial culture? Will they speak about how we were hostile to anything that we could not think of as a product to sell? Or, will it seem in hindsight like we just simply stayed indifferent to it all?

When we look back at the civilizations built by the Greeks and Romans, we marvel at their love of grandeur. We find ourselves inspired by their efforts to lift the aesthetic experience of entire populations. Think of the Colosseum or the Parthenon. Picture the great works of sculpture: the Venus de Milo or the bust of Marcus Aurelius. In contrast, we buy our art at discount department stores, and we construct the buildings we spend time in on the basis of a simple formula—we try to look for the lowest price per square foot.

With wild horses on public land in states like Wyoming, Nevada, and Utah, we are extraordinary, but without them we are not. Without them, we are Iowa. We need Iowa, of course. We need Kansas, Oklahoma, and Nebraska too. We need the whole breadbasket of America—maybe with fewer herbicides and pesticides—but we need food, and we need it on an industrial scale. Food is not enough, however. We need more. The Arizona-based essayist Charles Bowden suggested the following, with regard to our plight:

> *A lot of us have a hunger going on inside of us. We're not trying to regain our childhood or return to the glory of our*

high school years. We're storming out to find a new and better world, one we've never seen, have probably fabricated, and will most likely discover scraps of no matter how hard we search.

When it comes to the public places where we might conduct that search, it's the national parks that often come to mind. In the case of the parks, we protected important scraps of wildness. Today, throngs of people race through the cattle-grazed and flowerless prairies that separate city dwellers from places like Yosemite and Yellowstone. We travel to these locations because they provide us hope. They feel like our last best chance to experience terrain or an animal that represents the world the way it was. We visit the parks to look for something independent of us—landscapes and animals that exist outside the realm of commerce. In a 1983 article for *Wilderness*, Wallace Stegner described our parks as "the best idea we ever had … absolutely American … absolutely democratic." Today, relative to the size of the United States population, our parks are small and overcrowded.

We live in a time of change. The BLM's efforts to remove wild horses from the West serve the economic interests of a tiny number of agribusiness people, but they don't serve the common good. Eighty percent of us live in big American cities. By 2050, demographers predict that figure will rise to 90 percent. We are an increasingly urban population, turning our sights toward our last remaining examples of wild nature—for inspiration, health, and maybe even salvation. As the United States becomes increasingly urban, our interests in the outdoors, recreation, scenery, and wildlife expand.

In 2015, a record-setting number of Americans paid visits to national parks. Then in 2016, as a testimony to the rising level of interest in wildlife and the habitats where animals are found, we broke the record again. Visitation rates declined for a brief time in the era of the COVID-19 pandemic, but the parks stood poised to break all-time records again in the summer of 2021.

Are there too many wild horses? How many mustangs do we need? Like the late wilderness advocate Bob Marshall, I would answer these questions with a question: "How many Brahms' symphonies do we need?" The answer is, "All of them." We need big swaths of public grasslands with mustangs on them more than at any point in our history. We need their majesty and the adventure of striking out to try to find them. Wild horses also hold the potential to bring us together as a nation. Who among us wouldn't stop to marvel at the sight of a band of mustangs running through a rugged panorama in the West? They're one of the best ideas we have ever had ... highly American ... completely democratic.

By definition, and by law, wild horses are not for sale. After a roundup, the Bureau of Land Management allows qualified individuals to adopt mustangs, but we do not buy or sell them like domestic animals. They live outside of market forces and beyond the inequality and differences that tend to divide us. Wild horses belong to the wind, time, and the mystery of prairie grass seeds taking hold and pushing roots into the surface of the earth. But it turns out that's not enough. It hasn't been enough to keep government agencies from removing mustangs from their homes as a way to make room for livestock on our public land. As American values embedded in our policies, love of wildness and beauty did not do well in the twentieth century, and in truth, they haven't been faring too well lately. Even so, they are still the only values that can stand up to the force of economics.

STEPPES OF EVERLASTING BLISS

Ours is a time of great spiritual hunger. People are thirsting for the sacred, the mysterious, the mystical. They are looking for more than a good job, a full closet, and a balanced checkbook.

—John Michael Talbot, *The Lessons of Saint Francis*

Christ, what a sight to see a sagebrush desert with the horses still in it! Instead of a landscape dead under the sun, emptied of its life, this one crackles with drama.

—Dan Flores, *The Horizontal Yellow*

In the 1964 classic, *Totemism*, the anthropologist Claude Levi Strauss suggested, "Animals are good to think with." He made the comment after a career spent considering the norms, roles, and values of the groups native to central and southern America. On every continent, and all through time, animals have filled roles in our thoughts, our folklore, and our rituals. Among the Haida people of the Pacific Northwest, raven, eagle, and orca appear in stories as characters. In the contemporary United States, children nestle down at night with teddy bears, under dangly bee mobiles, and next to shelves lined with horse figurines. Parents read books to kids with animals embedded into scripts, real or imaginary. The stories contain timeless themes and considerations: *Curious George*, *Paddington Bear*, and *Black Beauty*, the well-known story of perseverance narrated by a horse.

Today, as in the past, we task each group and generation with creating a setting that allows children to build the skills and attitudes they'll need when they become adults. Despite iPads, nuclear power plants, and widespread urbanization, the human enterprise remains mostly unchanged. We use stories about forests, prairies, and animals to orient the young to the workings of the world. We introduce good and evil. We teach lessons about character, strength, and compassion. In *Words Are My Matter*, the novelist Ursula K. Le Guin explains, "Through story, every culture defines itself and teaches its children how to be people."

We tell our kids stories about animals and the habitats where they are found, and in so doing, we grind and shape the lens that they look through. We work to create in youth, an "environmental imagination," a vision and framework that guides them toward a way of seeing the earth and their relationship to the places where they live. Over time, our imaginations shape our consciousness. In the minds of adults, our imaginations and the views that flow from them provide texture to our daily existence. Then, of course, our day-to-day activities go on to shape the contents of the air we breathe, the quality of our waterways, the number and type of animals with whom we share our lives—even the look of the landscape itself.

⁓⁓⁓

But something happens in between a youth spent listening to stories about animals and adulthood. We send young kids to school. During our education, we learn that our futures require us to fulfill roles in the economy. For at least twelve years we please our teachers. In so doing, we learn how we might one day please a boss. We learn to sit quietly, listen, stand patiently, wait, do homework, and meet deadlines. We learn that each state in the union is endowed with its own set of resources and industries. In the East, we learn that mountaintops, if removed properly, reveal seams of sought-after coal. On the coasts, fishermen can trawl the ocean bottoms for a bounty of lobster. On the prairies of the West, cattlemen range their herds of black Angus and Herefords. Through the institution of education, we learn to see the world, and our role in this life, from the standpoint of the positions we might hold in the workforce.

The United States is a new nation compared to the cultures and countries of Asia or Africa. When European settlers landed on the east coast of the North American continent, they brought an expansionist frame of mind. White Europeans removed or displaced native people and animals wherever they conflicted with the landscapes they imagined as ideal for production. In the East, this meant the clearing of forests to make room for new cropland. In the Midwest, it involved the development of factories, and in the basins between the peaks and ranges of the West, ranchers saw large swaths of grass as a means to provide forage for cows and calves.

This tendency toward expansion fueled the physical makeover of North America, and by the late twentieth century, through the workings of the global marketplace, the earth. Stocks of cod and tuna dropped to dangerously low levels. People suffer the effects of poor air quality in cities around the globe, the chemicals of agriculture poison stores of freshwater, and the threat of rising seas looms over people living near coastlines. If that wasn't enough, life scientists predict a spike in extinctions to correspond with climate change, our desire for goods, and the loss of habitat that accompanies a lust for real estate.

In many ways, the basins of the West foretold the changes that would happen on a wider scale. As cattlemen approached the prairie, Eskimo curlews became extinct along with Audubon bighorns and Merriam's elk. Black-tailed prairie dog numbers dipped so low at the end of the twentieth century, biologists requested that politicians place them on the endangered species list. In the words of Dan Flores, from his book *The Horizontal Yellow*, "I still wonder at the mindset of it all, that mode of thinking that leads so thoughtlessly to extinguishing from the world the very elements that lend it grace, romance, and richness."

The pace of change moved quick across the prairie and over the continent. In the span of two generations, trees fell, cities rose, and rivers found themselves impounded behind the walls of dams. Here in the twenty-first century, however, we stand in a position that differs from that of our predecessors. Barring any unforeseen move to colonize other nations, or another planet, we possess all of the land mass that we can. Out of necessity, as Americans, we find our thoughts moving from expansion to the question of what comes next. Speaking from the year 1990, in his volume *The Experience of Place*, Tony Hiss suggested, "In the next 100 years or so, America will essentially complete itself." With our cities and infrastructures bending under the weight of time, and the rabid transformation of the North American landscape awfully close to complete, we find ourselves in a predicament. How do we live well in a wounded world that we helped to create?

During the last half of the twentieth century, the population of rural counties in the West began to shrink. It turns out that agribusinesses only provide a small number of job opportunities, and modest wages for employees. Predictably, young people raised in farm and ranching towns began to move to cities to look for new lives and careers. As a result of the decline in rural communities, and a well-documented tendency for cattle to overgraze and damage public land, two New Jersey–based academics, Frank and Deborah Popper, made a suggestion. From the halls of Rutgers University, they proposed that we take back parts of the public property that we lease to agribusinesses. They called the new region they envisioned the "Buffalo Commons." They advised federal officials, state governments, and county commissioners to identify suitable corridors, and then release bison back onto the prairies of the West. In the years that followed the proposal, they received death threats through the mail and over the telephone.

The Poppers only pointed out the obvious. Beef production on public land is a dubious undertaking. We offer grazing leases to a small group of agribusinesses at a rate so low it's widely thought of as a giveaway. The arrangement allows a small number of ranching enterprises to profit from our grasslands. In exchange, we permit cows to devour and trample the vegetation on public property. We let cattle foul our waterways with urine and feces, and we grant agribusiness people permission to shoot, trap, or poison any living thing that is not a cow or clump of forage. To a growing number of ecologists and commentators on public land, these patterns raise questions about what the American people lose as a result of the bargain that we've struck with the private parties we allow to ranch on the regions that we possess, together, as a nation.

In other countries, citizens and governments have cooperated to transform public land that has been stripped of wildlife into places where people can put themselves into contact with trees, grasses, and animals. In societies around the world, individuals and organizations are moving to create preserves where untamed beasts can thrive. In nations across the globe, people describe the process as "rewilding." In places where organizations take steps to rewild a landscape, horses often appear at the center of the effort.

In Mongolia, for example, a team of biologists worked to re-establish herds of Przewalski's horses—a subspecies once thought extinct. Their family tree has roots that extend back to the first group of equines that crossed from their birthplace in North America, across the Bering land bridge, to what is now Siberia. The Mongolian word for the animal is "takhi," which translates as "spirit" or "worthy of worship." The first time I heard the translation, I thought of a poem called "The Wild Divine" by Ada Limón. In a portion of the verse, she writes:

> *Out of the stoned-breath quiet of the hills,*
> *came another animal, a real animal, a wandering*
> *madrone-skinned horse [...]*
> *He rustled down his giant head to where we sat [...]*
> *he seemed almost worthy of complete devotion.*
> *We rubbed his long horse nose, his marble eyes turning*
> *to take us all in, to inhale us, to accept our now-selves*
> *and he was older, the wise-hooved big-hearted elder*
> *and I thought, this was what it was to be blessed—*
> *to know a love that was beyond an owning, beyond*

the body and its needs, but went straight from wild
thing to wild thing, approving of its wildness.[1]

In 1965, the entire population of takhi on earth included 134 horses, held mostly in European zoos. With the help of researchers from the Smithsonian, by the 1990s, the population had swelled to roughly 1,000. In the decade that followed, the nation of Mongolia underwent a transition toward democracy. Newly elected officials let the "spirit" of the nation loose upon the land, ending a century-long absence. Five previous generations could only read about takhi in books or hear about them in stories, but today, groups of schoolchildren visit reserves to view and study bands of wild horses.

Similarly, in 1968, conservationists and government agents in the Netherlands collaborated to create a 15,000-acre reserve for mammals, birds, and plants. They called the region the Oostvaardersplassen. A German magazine described the reserve as "the Serengeti behind the dikes." Under its initial plan, the Dutch reclaimed the land from the sea to provide new space for manufacturing, but something changed before they deeded the land to businesses. They decided to take part in a social movement: "Rewilding Europe." They committed to building a home for animals that were once removed or driven close to extinction.

With the help of American biologists, a team assessed the capacity of the space to provide habitat. The group settled on an initial release of 1,000 wild horses, long since missing from the Dutch landscape. They also released a group of bovines called Heck

---

[1] From *Bright Dead Things* by Ada Limon (Minneapolis: Milkweed Editions, 2015). Copyright (c) 2015 by Ada Limon. Reprinted with permission from Milkweed Editions. milkweed.org

cows. Heck cattle share ancestry with aurochs, the wild predecessors of today's livestock. Not long after the large animals began to graze the grass of the reserve—foxes, muskrats, and red deer arrived on their own. Then attendants began to record sightings of eagles, goshawks, kestrels, kingfishers, and a rare example of a black buzzard. Today, travelers and educational groups pay a forty-dollar fee to take a tour of the Oostvaardersplassen.

.⁂.▾▴.☸.▴▾.⁂.

The rewilding efforts that have taken place in Europe and Asia are right and good. Yet, as a pragmatist, I am reluctant to suggest a widespread plan to rewild a large portion of the United States. First, I am not keen to court any death threats. Then there's my skepticism about plans to return the earth or big parts of it to a state that existed prior to the Industrial Revolution. Moving the hands of the clock backward would pose a challenge. Pure buffalo, with no domestic cow genes, are tough to find. The passenger pigeon went extinct. Plus, over time, we changed things in ways that I appreciate: the brown trout from Germany that swim in Rocky Mountain streams, for example. Or the ring-necked pheasants we imported from Asia. In North America, any honest attempt to rewild the place would require us to return large tracts of land to Native people. That's a move that I could support, but it's one that continues to meet opposition.

The conservationist Bill McKibben often explains that we're not likely going to get back the planet we used to have. In a 2019 article for *Time* magazine called "Hello from the Year 2050," he suggested, even if we avoid the worst effects of climate change, in less than three decades, we will find a situation where "Everything is different." When he made the point, he did not do so as a way to signal regret. Neither our personal happiness nor the health of the planet depends on our ability to return parts of our habitat to a historic state, not when the present is full of wonder and the future still holds potential. At the moment, we have a policy on the books that originally protected wild horses in 339 herd areas across ten US states. I would feel glad if we just upheld the law.

The policy contains a key flaw, however. The federal Wild and Free-Roaming Horses and Burros Act grants the Bureau of Land Management the sole authority to determine the number of mustangs we allow on public property. That's a lot of power to place in the hands of the BLM. For each herd area, the agency sets what they call an "appropriate management level" under the acronym AML. The AML represents the official number of mustangs that can roam free on the land we set aside for them. In the time since the passage of the Wild Horses and Burros Act, the BLM has set "zero" as the appropriate number of mustangs in 162 of the 339 herd areas initially protected at the federal level—a total loss of habitat that approaches 50 percent.

Even at that, some states fared better than others as the Bureau moved to shrink the space available to horses. In Wyoming, for example, mustangs were initially protected in forty-four different herd areas. Today, horses are present in just sixteen of those, and the BLM recently published a plan to make "zero" the appropriate number of wild horses in two additional Wyoming herds. In each case where the BLM "zeroes out" a group of mustangs, private herds of sheep and cattle graze—hard at work—chewing their way over the landscape.

⠄⠢⠈⠢⠈⠈⠢⠈⠢⠄

What about us? At times, I wonder, "Are we any different from sheep? Or cattle?" Have we become single-mindedly bent on serving the global economy? In the United States, cultural forces encourage us to find a lane on what sociologists describe as a "work-to-spend" treadmill. We work fifty out of fifty-two weeks a year, so we can live in admirable houses and fill them with objects that other members of society approve.

Wild mustangs are the perfect creatures to help relieve us from a one-dimensional worldview, where everyone and everything is reduced to their value in the marketplace. In *Frederick Remington's Own West*, the artist, always fond of the mustang as a subject, describes the wild horse as a "living protest against utilitarianism." Similarly, in *Cowboy Ethics*, James P. Owen cites a cherished American value: "Some things aren't for sale."

Travelers bring money with them when they visit states with bands of wild horses, and research suggests that they spend ample amounts while they're away from home. Outside of the revenue generated through tourism, however, mustangs serve no economic purpose. When herds of wild horses numbered in the millions, we harvested them as meat products. Today, ten states host herds that number in the hundreds or thousands, and if we harvested them with any kind of intent, they'd vanish within a week or two. In our culture, we do not hunt horses. We don't eat them, they no longer pull our plows, and they are too expensive for most of us to own and keep. In other words, they fall outside our normal obsession with economics. They are the perfect beasts to help us make our flat lives three-dimensional.

We are the storytelling creatures on this good, green earth. We capture and manage our existence through the process of crafting narratives. We set our life stories in a place and then we look for ways to add meaning. We incorporate events that help us to recollect: where we came from, who we are, and the directions that we hope to go. Encounters with raw landscapes and creatures that exist outside of society give us occasion to pause and add memorable chapters to the stories that we tell and retell to confirm our sense of self. Such encounters also provide us with a way to measure ourselves against the world. They give us the chance to compare ourselves to other forms of life. It's educational. When we put ourselves in a position where our lives press up against others, we make judgments. By comparison, do we like what we see?

In 1846, Henry David Thoreau took part in a failed bid to climb Mount Kahtadin, the highest peak in the state of Maine. Midway through the endeavor, heavy fog clouded the route. It made the woods impassable. The weather turned the party back before they made it to the summit. On the descent, Thoreau found himself attempting to navigate a forest of brambles dark enough to limit his vision. To describe the place, he wrote:

> *This was the earth of which we have heard, made out of Chaos and Old Night. Here was no [human's] garden, but the unhandled globe. It was not lawn, nor pasture, nor mead, nor woodland, nor lea, nor arable, nor wasteland.*

It was Matter, vast, terrific ... rocks, trees, wind on our cheeks! The solid earth! The actual world! The common sense! Contact! Contact! Who are we?

Who, indeed. What have we become? These are questions of considerable size. Most of the time, they are too big. They're not the sort of topics we can give thought to when we are caught in the whorl of daily life.

The American sociologist C. Wright Mills described each of our days as an array of traps. In *The Sociological Imagination*, Mills explained how the demands of making a living and raising a family present us with a rapidly unfolding series of distractions. Monday through Friday, commitments unspool in front of us. They hold us down in the tumult. Even Thoreau admitted, in an essay about walking in the woods, he found it difficult to "shake off the village."

It is tough to find time or a way to ponder the question of who we are with any rigor. It's hard to carve enough space out of our busy lives to analyze the forces that work on us—shaping our traits and desires. Most of the time, we're forced to simply chisel at our to-do lists. Thoreau discovered that exceptional moments give us the power to transcend the more mundane aspects of life. The Hermit of Walden understood how the experience of nature can lift us to a place where we can look back and make judgments with respect to the character of our existence.

We give Thoreau and his colleague Ralph Waldo Emerson credit for launching what we call the transcendental movement of the nineteenth century—a uniquely American, and uniquely historic approach to life and philosophy. Still, the human compulsion to transcend is timeless. The act of breaking through the ceiling of daily life has roots in tribal arrangements where shamanism and ritual dance released people from the bonds of day-to-day expectations. From shamanism all the way to Starbucks and online shopping for electronics, we have been looking for a means to give ourselves a lift. In a passage from his title, *The Solace of Fierce Landscapes*, the theologian Belden Lane tells us, "We never tire of the effort to … possess ideal states of consciousness."

An unfenced swath of prairie, graced by the hoofbeats of horses, serves as a ladder that leads to transcendence. Free-roaming bands of mustangs remind us that this country of ours is still wild, and thus, we are at least a little wild too. We're something other than just workers. We are more than individuals pursuing our self-interest. We are a people who, as a nation, made it official policy to protect something big, untamed, and majestic. A band of wild horses on a stretch of our grasslands acts like a stained-glass window, bending and giving color to the light of creation.

At Casper College, I teach an introduction to world religions. We offer the class every semester. The available seats often fill up even though the course is not specifically required in any degree programs. Some students bring an ardent form of Christianity to class, hoping to learn the features of other religions as a way to argue in favor of their own. Committed atheists sometimes sign up for the course too. They usually use the class as a way to test the mettle of their choice, with regard to the denial of something larger or sacred at work in the cosmos. But I would describe the majority of my students as "honest seekers." In the Pew Research Center's ongoing study of American religiosity, today's generation of college students is among the most likely to identify themselves as "spiritual, but not religious." It's the fastest-growing category in the Pew Center's survey, and it represents our current search and sense of restlessness.

Many commentators have remarked upon the spiritual hunger of our age. Who among us hasn't looked up from the screen of a handheld device to wonder if there isn't something more? Something immense? Profound? Significant? I might even describe our state as one of narrative hunger, borne of an understanding that a role in the United States economy and the shrunken worldview that stems from time spent screen-scrolling are not wholly sufficient. Every year, every semester, I watch students select majors, seek new identities, and chart the early chapters in their life stories. They wear their trepidations like a set of clothes. They know the magnitude of their choices. They understand how one wrong move can put them on a path toward a lengthy, drab, and meaningless adulthood. Without ever having read Henry David Thoreau, young people know the potential for our economy to set them on a course toward a life of "quiet desperation."

Today's generation of college students entered the world roughly at the time of the attacks on the World Trade Center in New York: September 11, 2001. They watched their parents weather the effects of the Great Recession. Throughout their lives, they witnessed as a changing climate ravaged their homes with fires and floods. They've been the victims of school shootings. As they came of age, the entire population of the planet faced the threat of a global pandemic, and on January 6, 2021, we all watched as an angry mob stormed the United States Capitol, smashing windows and calling into question the values and convictions that ensure peace in democracies. In his 1919 poem "The Second Coming," William Butler Yeats made what now feels like a prescient declaration: "*Things fall apart; the centre cannot hold / … the ceremony of innocence is drowned / the best lack all conviction, while the worst/are full of passionate intensity.*"

For tens of thousands of years, in nations across the globe, previous generations enjoyed the benefit of well-set bulwarks standing up against the twin threats of apathy and pessimism. Throughout most of human history, each society conducted rite-of-passage ceremonies, meant to weave young people into the fabric of their culture. Those rites of passage involved lessons from elders on the role of adult men and women, in both social life and in relation to the natural world. In the rites that still remain, the Jewish bar and bat mitzvahs, for example, scriptures offer hope and a guide for making ethical choices. In most eras of our past, however, we found meaning in constellations. The appearance of wild animals in one's daily life held importance and offered occasions for reflection. We taught each other to know our places to the same degree that we know ourselves.

In my classes, I have an activity that I conduct every year. I show students examples of corporate logos with a projector. One at a time, logos flash on a screen at the front of the room: Apple, Facebook, Instagram, Nike, McDonalds, and Chevrolet. I ask students to identify each image. Out loud, we shout the names of the corporations that the logos represent. Then I begin to place images of local trees onto the screen: elm, pine, fir, oak, and cottonwood. The room stays quiet as the images come and go, but we all raise our eyebrows in speculation about how far we have drifted. Then I admit that I couldn't tell the difference between a spruce or fir until after I turned thirty. That helps takes the edge off a moment with potential for awkwardness.

In a discussion with Thomas Clarke, published under the title *Befriending the Earth*, the theologian Thomas Berry explains, "We are talking only to ourselves ... we are not talking to the rivers, we are not listening to the wind and the stars, we have broken the great conversation." In short, we tend to limit our emotional participation in nature's mystery. Too often, we forget to practice the art of beholding. We've largely forgotten what it means to attend to our environment.

In the languages of North America's indigenous people, our state translates as "soul loss," a disorder that occurs when we fail to recognize the sacredness in nature. It's a common condition, one where the world around us turns into a set of resources, simply waiting outside our doors, unacknowledged, until the time when we find occasion to harness a piece of our habitat for use in the economy.

Our immediate communication with nature has waned, creating a kind of spiritual poverty that allows us to destroy a world that previous societies held in reverence. In the poem "The World Is Too Much with Us," William Wordsworth suggested, "*Getting and spending we lay waste our powers / little we see in nature that is ours / we have given our hearts away.*" Maybe so, but our imaginations still yearn for a geography to provide us with meaning, a setting on which to craft the stories that turn into our lives.

Even for those of us out of practice when it comes to adoring our habitat, the sight of wild horses on a prairie landscape full of sage leads to feelings of awe toward creation—almost every single time. In the words of the Flathead people of Montana, mustangs serve as an example of "big medicine," and they're the medicine we need at this stage in our history. They open up the gate. They are enchanting—right in the middle of a mostly disenchanted world of commerce, technology, and a torrent of bids for our time-shortened spans of attention.

At the point when we were first beginning to conceive national parks like Yellowstone and Yosemite, John Muir observed, "Thousands of tired, nerve-shaken, over-civilized people are beginning to find out that … wildness is a necessity." From his place in the past, Muir had no way to confirm the profound accuracy of his observation. Perhaps, if he were alive today, it would not surprise Muir to see more than three quarters of a million people passing through the gates of Yellowstone National Park every month, from May to September. He saw the future. As a native of the Midwest, Muir bore witness to the march of agriculture and industry across the heart of the continent. He watched as our enterprises logged forests and overturned prairies. Rather than take part in the taming of nature in the middle of the nation, Muir headed west. Then from his home at the base of the Sierra Range, he began to use his vision and a pen to harvest the best crops left in North America—beauty and wildness.

Of course, we depend on farms and factories. In the end, however, they do not provide enough. In *Wilderness Sojourn*, David Douglas said it better than I could when he described the best crop or product that a place can offer its people: "silence and solitude, a sense of awe and gratitude, able to be harvested by anyone who visits."

In the regions of the nation presided over by the Bureau of Land Management, we find opportunities to hear silence and experience solitude. Sprinkled across the West, set on tracts of BLM land, we also find horse herd management areas, and here we add the chance to feel both gratitude and awe—mustangs caring for their foals, squinting into one another's eyes, or running full-tilt across open ground. None of us will ever make a living by staring at families of wild horses, but as long as mustangs roam our public grasslands, I expect they will continue to help us complete our lives.

APPENDIX I:
DECONSTRUCTING WILD HORSE MYTHS

Myth #1: Mustangs Are Overpopulated in the West

It's the staff of the Bureau of Land Management that determines the number of mustangs permitted to live in the nation's wild horse herd areas. In 2019, the BLM set 26,700 as the maximum number allowed, as a way to maintain what the agency considers an appropriate management level (AML), across the ten western states with current herds. On this subject, in May of 2020, the BLM published *An Analysis of Achieving a Sustainable Wild Horse and Burro Program*. In the report, the authors outline the steps the Bureau is taking to reduce our wild horse population to 26,700.

In a 1959 estimate for *Geographical Review*, Thomas McKnight estimated that 2 to 5 million mustangs roamed the West, historically. An AML of 26,700 represents at least a 98.7 percent decrease in the number of wild horses in the United States. That figure alone would likely justify a listing of the American mustang as threatened under the terms of the Endangered Species Act, but it's the loss of genetic diversity that represents the greatest risk to the long-term presence and stability of wild horse populations. According to the International Union for the Conservation of Nature (IUCN), a species becomes threatened when its range is limited to "restricted populations" of less than

"250 adults." Of the original 339 wild horse herd areas identified in 1971, at present, 308 of those areas have AMLs set at less than 250 horses. In other words, 90 percent of our original mustang herds have either been eliminated or pressed into restricted quarters where potential for inbreeding threatens the health of future generations.

At times, wild horse populations in the West are cited as an "out-of-control problem." Such claims result from mustang numbers rising above the management levels set by the BLM. The claims are not based on an analysis of the number of wild horses that a region can support, however. It is important to keep in mind that livestock outnumber mustangs on our public lands by ratios that range from 92:1 to 28:1, depending on the year and location. When the BLM implements fertility control programs for mustangs, or when they round up and remove wild horses, in effect, they are reducing the number of free-roaming equines as a way to make room for the larger herds of private sheep and cattle the agency permits on our public property.

Consider New Mexico. The BLM manages wild horses in two different herd areas in the northern and central parts of the state. The areas provide horses with access to 29,000 acres of public land. In the two combined herds, the agency has set the AML at a total of 83 animals. If the population should happen to rise up to 166, double the AML, that's still short of the number needed to assure enough diversity to avoid birth defects and long-term genetic decline. Even so, critics might charge, "There are twice as many mustangs as our rangelands can support!" In truth, if the population of New Mexico mustangs rose to 2,900, that would still afford each horse enough space to graze 1,000 acres each.

On their own, at present numbers, science does not suggest that wild horses threaten the ecosystems where they're found. It is rarely science that underlies our decisions about wildlife and the use of public lands, however. According to the BLM's own documents, specifically, the *Report of the Review Team on Forage Allocations for Wild Horses and Livestock*, the ultimate decision on the balance between mustangs and cattle is a "social and political one," based on "perceptions and values." When wild horse detractors claim, "There are too many mustangs!" it is crucial to remember that these are not statements of fact, but rather, declarations of bias—toward domestic stock and in opposition to wild, free-roaming animals.

Myth #2: Wild Horses Harm Public Grasslands

The prairies and basins overseen by the Bureau of Land Management are often overgrazed. In a 2018 testimony before the House Natural Resources Subcommittee on Public Lands, members of the group, Public Employees for Environmental Responsibility, testified to the effect that 30 percent of the lands managed by the BLM do not meet the agency's standards for a sustainable and healthy range. They went on to explain that 70 percent of the damage is a result of commercial livestock grazing.

Government agencies allow cattle to occupy 251 million acres of our public land, and in contrast, we permit wild horses and burros on a total of 29.4 million acres. In other words, in a given year, we could potentially find wild horses on no more than 12 percent of the property overseen by the Forest Service and Bureau of Land Management. Critics of the Wild Horse and Burro program often point to the presence of mustangs or wild burros as an explanation for the grim state of our grasslands. Such claims serve as an example of scapegoating. When it comes to explaining the problem of overgrazed and unhealthy grasslands, the explanation leans in only one direction: agribusiness.

Myth #3: Mustangs Are an Invasive Species (Non-Native)

The modern horse evolved in North America. The earliest fossil records date back more than 55 million years. Due to abundant skeletal remains, archeologists can easily delineate the evolution of the horse, all the way from the "dawn pony," the original herbivore, to *Equus caballus,* the creature that we know today. On this continent, we find strong evidence of horses present in large numbers—from their starting point in the Eocene—up until the most recent discovery, a sample of 5,000-year-old horse DNA uncovered from the soil in the Yukon Territory. The genetic material, collected by a team headquartered at McMaster University, established that the historic North American DNA matches that of the modern horse.

In late 2021, the university released a report under the title, "Ancient DNA found in soil samples reveals mammoths, Yukon wild horses survived thousands of years longer than believed." The report contains an unequivocal statement from a partner on the project, Ross MacPhee, Senior Curator in the Department of Mammalogy at the American Museum of Natural History. According to MacPhee, "The horse that lived in the Yukon 5,000 years ago is directly related to the horse species we have today, *Equus caballus.* Biologically, this makes the horse a native North American mammal, and it should be treated as such."

Like most large creatures in the time of the last ice age, horses migrated from North America into Asia, and then they either vanished from this continent or they saw their populations shrink. Some new evidence suggests that Native American tribes possessed carvings of horse figurines circa 1500, and new data on the genetics of Appaloosas suggest that they migrated, or were brought back, to North America from Asia at a time that's still unknown. Without question, 500 years ago, Spanish explorers loaded horses onto ships, returned them to their home, and set them free. Until we find a set of horse remains that are 2,000 or 800 years old, it is still questionable, but perhaps fair to assume that horses went regionally extinct and remained so for roughly 4,500 years.

To put this into perspective, if we could reduce the 55-million-year history of horses in America to a single 24-hour period, for the sake of illustration, horses would be present on this continent for the first 23 hours, 59 minutes, and 43 seconds. They would disappear for the last 17 ticks of the clock. Then they would return at the end of the day. Under such circumstances, is there any way to consider them out of place? If horses are not native to the North American continent, then where are they indigenous? The mustangs of the West are often described as a non-native species, but that characterization is dishonest.

Horses evolved in North America. It is possible that they disappeared here for a short time. Then human beings brought them home. The situation is similar to the one we find in the National Parks. For example, in the Badlands of South Dakota, bison and bighorn sheep were both eliminated from the landscape by the middle 1800s. Then in the twentieth century, field biologists trapped specimens in other areas and relocated them to the Badlands, where they once lived in large numbers. This scenario is no different from the one we find in the case of wild horses.

Myth #4: Wild Horses Are "Feral"

A feral animal is one that lives independently after leaving a domestic setting. Genetic testing has confirmed that the wild horses of the West trace their lineage to a set of ancestors brought to this continent by Spanish explorers. Wild horses in the West also possess genetic markers traceable to United States cavalry troops and herds maintained by tribes of Native people in the time when they controlled the plains. In addition, farm and ranch horses are occasionally turned out onto public land, and some of those animals fall in with bands of mustangs. Apart from the last example, if you have the good luck to see a wild horse in the United States, there is a strong chance that you would have to trace the animal's genealogy back through as many as five centuries before you reach an ancestor that had served as a partner to a person. Does that make them feral? Of course not.

Sometimes anglers make a distinction between wild and hatchery-raised fish, but as soon as a generation of trout are born in the wild—they are wild. The same is true with regard to horses.

Myth #5: Mustangs Are Malnourished

In some parts of the West, in periods of drought, horses become malnourished, just like any other animal that forages for food.

Cases of undernourished or emaciated mustangs are unique and isolated, however. Most often, mustangs appear too thin to Americans because we grow accustomed to spending time with domestic horses. Our domestic animals are a lot like us—they're soft and round. They eat too much, and because they live in spaces defined by the size of our real estate, they are unable to exercise. In contrast, wild horses run. Mustangs are like the athletes among us. They are lean. Sometimes their bodies appear chiseled. In some cases, when summer coats are thin, their ribs show through. Most often, however, these are signs of fitness as opposed to starvation.

Myth #6: Wild Horses Have No Natural Predators

On its web pages, and in print, the Bureau of Land Management makes a regular claim to the effect that "the wild horse has no natural predators." In truth, through the nineteenth and twentieth centuries, by means of trapping, hunting, and poison, we exterminated most of the large predators on the North American continent. Historically, wolves and grizzly bears preyed on mustangs. Today, we find no overlap between wild horse herd areas and bear or wolf habitat. But one large carnivore remains—the mountain lion. For millions of years, lions stalked bands of horses across our mountains and prairies. Likewise, in current reports from wildlife biologists, we find a growing body of data on the number of mustangs eaten by cougars.

In herd areas as far flung as Arizona and Montana, horses and mountain lions maintain a working predator–prey relationship. In parts of Nevada, field scientists have discovered cougars with diets that consist almost entirely of mustangs. The big cats tend to prey on foals, although not exclusively, and they eat horses at a rate of roughly one every other week. When it comes to the question of how to create stable mustang populations, we find a scientific consensus on the idea that natural predation offers an important strategy. The only question still unanswered is the one about whether we can find the political will or cultural resolve to protect an ample number of lions.

Myth #7: Mustangs Compete with Other Forms of Wildlife

Wild horses coexist well with a wide range of herbivores. As a photographer, I've captured images of mustangs grazing side by side with elk, pronghorn, and mule deer. Through human eyes, they actually appear to enjoy mixed company. The relationship between horses and other herbivores is more directly beneficial, however. In the winter, horses use their strength and weight to break the ice on frozen creeks and ponds. In so doing, they keep water open and available for smaller animals like deer and antelope. In addition, when mustangs eat grass, the seeds pass through their bodies and return to the ground as a component of their manure. As a result, horses reseed the regions where they graze—a boon to all of the animals that depend upon grasses.

APPENDIX II:
MUSTANG GROUPS AND RESCUE CENTERS

Advocate's Associations

In the time since the passing of the Wild and Free-Roaming Horses and Burros Act, equine advocates across the nation have created a range of nonprofit groups. Many of the organizations serve as watchdogs, overseeing the management practices of the government officials charged with protecting our mustangs. These groups and their members attend BLM roundups and film the proceedings to ensure the agency adheres to humane practices. These groups also organize letter-writing campaigns, and they use online resources as a way to educate and inspire new generations of activists.

Starting Points for Groups to Consult or Support:
American Wild Horse Campaign
americanwildhorsecampaign.org

Over the course of its history, the American Wild Horse Campaign has become one of the nation's most effective advocacy groups. The organization works to educate the public and legislators on the advantages of managing wild horse populations with doses of the fertility control drug PZP, administered in the field. The group also promotes wild horse herd management areas as sites for ecotourism, with the understanding that the argument for maintaining robust herds of wild horses often rests, in part, on the ability to make the case that wildlife contributes to regional economies.

The Cloud Foundation

thecloudfoundation.org

The Cloud Foundation is another effective organization, fighting for fair allocations of forage in wild horse habitat, an end to roundups, and the use of humane, reversible fertility control. TCF's namesake is a stallion from the Pryor Mountain Range on the border of Wyoming and Montana. The group's founder, Emmy Award–winning producer, Ginger Kathrens, shot and directed a series of films about the horse and the region, beginning with the PBS/Nature special, *Cloud: Wild Stallion of the Rockies*. The Cloud Foundation staff maintain updates on their website, along with links to educational material and information about how horse advocates can best contact legislators and donate time as volunteers.

Friends of a Legacy (FOAL)

friendsofalegacy.org

The FOAL organization serves as an example of a local effort to cooperate with federal agencies to ensure the welfare of wild horses. The group, based in Cody, Wyoming, works with the Bureau of Land Management to orchestrate a program where the wild mares in the McCollough Peaks herd receive regular doses of the fertility-control serum PZP. The program allows FOAL and the BLM to maintain the herd's population size with a high level of long-term stability. The McCollough Peaks mustangs seldom require roundups. The horses live out their lives on the range. In addition, FOAL members worked with the BLM to construct a series of interpretive signs, making visits to see the horses of the McCollough Peaks area fruitful, even for newcomers to the region.

North Dakota Badlands Horse
ndbh.org

The members of the North Dakota Badlands Horse organization devote their attention to the preservation and promotion of wild horses in Theodore Roosevelt National Park. As a component of their efforts, the group tracks, records, and documents the presence of the park's mustangs for the purpose of maintaining a registry. The registry allows visitors to identify horses, and in addition, the records allow adopters to know each animal's five-generation pedigree.

Pryor Mountain Wild Mustang Center
pryormustangs.org

Located in Lovell, Wyoming, the Pryor Mountain Wild Mustang Center is a natural stop for anyone aiming to visit the federally designated Pryor Mountain Wild Horse Range. The center provides a unique visitor's facility, along the route to mustang habitat. The staff offers tours of the likely places to find wild horses, and the organization also publishes annual guides to the mustangs that make their home in the region.

Western Horse Watcher's Association
westernhorsewatchers.com

Under the leadership of Brendan Duffy, an engineer by training, Western Horse Watchers monitor the decisions made by the Bureau of Land Management. In particular, they document, and make public, a record of the BLM's land use decisions inside wild horse herd areas. When information on the BLM's practices becomes available, Western Horse Watchers publishes the data online, so concerned citizens can see and consider the differences between the size of wild horse and livestock populations on our public lands.

Wild Beauty Foundation
wildbeautyfoundation.org

The Wild Beauty Foundation was founded by Ashley Avis, the director of Disney's most recent adaptation of Anna Sewell's *Black Beauty*. Through the use of a unique film and entertainment platform, the WBF works to raise awareness of the threats faced by American mustangs. Specifically, the foundation's work is aimed at putting an end to helicopter roundups, the separation of bonded equine families, and the existence of mass holding facilities for horses removed from their homes on our public land.

Wild Horse Education
wildhorseeducation.org

Laura Leigh curates the Wild Horse Education website. Leigh was among the first videographers to attend and record footage of the roundups conducted by the Bureau of Land Management. Her organization's website includes links to an annual reading room, information for beginning mustang viewers, and links to web pages where citizens can take action in support of wild horses.

Wild Horse Freedom Federation

wildhorsefreedomfederation.org

The Wild Horse Freedom Federation engages in a range of activities, all directed toward the preservation of mustangs and burros on public land. The website listed above contains links to news and alerts. The Federation also takes legal action in cases where the Bureau of Land Management violates the terms of the Wild and Free-Roaming Horses and Burros Act. In addition, the group produces the Wild Horse and Burro Radio program, available for streaming online through a link on the group's homepage.

Wild Hoofbeats

wildhoofbeats.com

The Wild Hoofbeats website is maintained by the award-winning conservation photographer Carol Walker. The site contains a link to Walker's blog where she posts regular updates on the politics and management of wild horses. The site also serves as a retail outlet for Walker's books. In the case of titles such as *Galloping to Freedom*, she chronicles her involvement with observing and protecting bands of mustangs. In addition, her volume *Horse Photography* offers a practical guide for beginning photographers interested in making high-quality images. The site also hosts a set of links to white papers, reports, and other materials.

Wild Horses of America Foundation

wildhorses.org

Kamas, Utah, is the base of operations for the Wild Horses of America Foundation. The organization focuses its activities primarily on the mustangs still allowed to roam free in the group's home state. The foundation is also committed to the long-term, humane management of the BLM's Onaqui herd, located in northern Utah.

Sanctuaries and Rescue Organizations

In the 1980s, it became clear that BLM staff had committed to a strategy of rounding up and removing mustangs from their homes. The frequent roundups created a need for a new type of organization. Today, across the country, dedicated women and men maintain equine rescue operations. In every case, the groups have worked to secure enough property to ensure that a portion of the horses taken from public land can spend what remains of their lives in a setting where they enjoy some level of freedom. Most nonprofit rescue ranches offer tours, and like their sister groups focused on advocacy, rescue centers also work to increase public awareness of wild horse issues.

A Short List of Rescue Centers or Sanctuaries to Visit:
The Black Hills Wild Horse Sanctuary
wildmustangs.com

The Black Hills Wild Horse Sanctuary is nestled at the bottom of a valley along a stretch of the Cheyenne River, south of Hot Springs, South Dakota. The sanctuary was founded by the author and naturalist Dayton Hyde. The facility and property serve as a home for rescued horses with clear Spanish bloodlines, along with specimens uniquely bred by Native American tribes. In 2019, after a long history of providing lodging and adventure tours, the sanctuary temporarily closed its doors to public visitation, but the organization still makes it possible for individuals to sponsor rescued horses, and goods from the sanctuary's gift shop are accessible online.

Deerwood Ranch Wild Horse EcoSanctuary

deerwoodranchwildhorseecosanctuary.com

The location of Deerwood Ranch is convenient to visitors of Laramie or Centennial, Wyoming. The ranch provides a home for more than 300 mustangs rescued from BLM holding corrals. The staff provide public tours of the property, ranch facilities are available to host events, and visitors have the option of renting a guest cabin.

Great Escape Mustang Sanctuary & Training Center

greatescapesanctuary.org

The Great Escape organization is housed on a 900-acre ranch outside of Deer Trail, Colorado. In addition to providing a home for rescued mustangs, Great Escape also serves as host of an "on the range" group, the Sand Wash Advocacy Team (SWAT). The sanctuary's SWAT team works with Bureau of Land Management officials in northern Colorado to provide fertility control and gather support for the state's Sand Wash Basin herd management area. At the ranch, Great Escape also offers public lodging for visitors and guests.

Lifesavers Wild Horse Rescue

wildhorserescue.org

Based in Caliente, California, Lifesavers provides a home for hundreds of mustangs that were at one time threatened by starvation or the potential for slaughter. The organization fills two roles. The first is to maintain a preserve for the horses that they rescue. Second, the group's staff works to gentle select animals, so they can become successful adoptees. As part of their gentling and adoption practices, Lifesavers also conducts workshops for students interested in learning about the practice of horse training.

Montana's Wild Horse Sanctuary and Guest Ranch
montanaswildhorses.org

Montana's Wild Horse Sanctuary provides a home for rescued mustangs on a 1,600-acre ranch outside of Helena. In addition to serving as a home for displaced horses, sanctuary staff also take steps to gentle and train their residents in order to ensure safe and successful adoptions.

Montgomery Creek Mustangs
montgomerycreekranch.org

The Montgomery Creek ranch provides a 2,000-acre sanctuary for more than 200 rescued horses in northern California. The staff of the ranch specialize in preparing young mustangs for adoption. The Montgomery Creek Ranch's founder Ellie Phipps Price was the impetus behind the creation of *American Mustang: The Movie*, a full-length documentary film. The ranch also hosts a series of horse-gentling workshops and clinics throughout the year.

Skydog Ranch and Sanctuary
skydogranch.org

Skydog Ranch maintains properties in Bend, Oregon, and Malibu, California. The Oregon ranch is set in a rural area. The location hosts hundreds of rescued horses and burros, including many reunited families separated during roundups. In southern California, Skydog uses its property to educate the public on issues that relate to wild horse conservation. The group's staff focus their energy on purchasing mustangs that have been sold to buyers intending to send the animals to slaughter. Skydog staff monitor the stockyards of auctioneers, and in many cases, they rescue mustangs and burros from off of trailers bound for meatpacking facilities.

Sky Mountain Wild Horse Sanctuary
skymountainwild.org

The Sky Mountain Wild Horse Sanctuary offers homes for mustangs rounded up and removed from public land in their home state and location—New Mexico. In addition to providing homes for displaced animals, the organization also works to increase the use of fertility-control serum as an alternative to mustang removal and long-term storage. They concentrate their efforts on the bands of wild horses that remain in the Southwest, the Carson National Forest, specifically.

Sweetbeau Horses
sweetbeauhorses.org

Located on California's central coast, near the city of Paso Robles, Sweetbeau offers an intensive gentling process for formerly free-ranging mustangs. The goal of the organization is to train rescued horses at a high level of skill, to help ensure successful adoptions and the establishment of safe, permanent homes for the animals. In addition, the group's mission also includes plans to make use of the property and facility as an equine therapy center and retreat for victims of post-traumatic stress.

Wild Horse Sanctuary

wildhorsesanctuary.org

As part of its mission, the Wild Horse Sanctuary staff conduct pack trips. They also offer public education programs, and they sponsor "resistance free" horse training seminars—all from a 5,000-acre preserve in Shingletown, California. The sanctuary operates as a working model for the responsible management of wild horses in a natural and balanced habitat. Deer, black bears, bobcats, and wild turkeys live in the company of mustangs. The site is open to visitors without a reservation on Wednesdays and Saturdays.

Wild Love Preserve

wildlovepreserve.org

The Wild Love Preserve opened in 2010 with a group of 136 mustangs removed from the Challis Idaho Herd Management Area. The preserve provides a home for mustangs, and the organization also works collaboratively with both the BLM and private landowners. In addition to the sanctuary, Wild Love also partners with a tour company called Seeks Out Adventures. The tour group offers guided trail rides and overnight pack trips in Idaho's wild horse herd management areas.

Wind River Wild Horse Sanctuary

windriverwildhorses.com

The Wind River Wild Horse Sanctuary blends a mustang rescue facility with a visitor center, museum, and tours designed to educate the public on issues that relate to both mustang and Native American history. Located on the Wind River Reservation, west of Lander, Wyoming, the sanctuary offers free access to its educational resources during regular business hours, along with privately guided tours available for a minimal fee.

APPENDIX III:
SOURCES AND SUGGESTIONS FOR FURTHER EXPLORATION

Amaral, Anthony. 1977. *Mustang*. Reno: University of Nevada Press.

Animal Welfare Institute. 2011. *Managing for Extinction: Shortcomings of the Bureau of Land Management's National Wild Horse and Burro Program*. Washington, DC: Animal Welfare Institute.

Behnke, Robert J. 1977. "Grazing and the Riparian Zone: Impact on Aquatic Values." United States Forest Service. Retrieved from: https://tinyurl.com/mvmncj9p.

Bekoff, Marc. 2014. *Rewilding Our Hearts: Building Pathways of Compassion and Coexistence*. New York: New World Books.

Berger, Joel. 1986. *Wild Horses of the Great Basin*. Chicago: University of Chicago Press.

Budiansky, Stephen. 1977. *The Nature of Horses: Exploring Equine Evolution, Intelligence, and Behavior*. New York: Simon & Schuster.

Bureau of Land Management. 1996. *Report of the Review Team on Forage Allocations for Wild Horses and Livestock*. Washington, DC: United States Department of the Interior.

———. 2020. *Report to Congress: An Analysis of Achieving a Sustainable Wild Horse and Burro Program*. Washington, DC: United States Department of the Interior.

Cruise, David, and Alison Griffiths. 2013. *Wild Horse Annie and the Last of the Mustangs: The Life of Velma Johnston.* New York: Scribner.

Curtin, Sharon, John Eastcott, and Yva Momatiuk. 1996. *Mustang.* Bearsville, NY: Rufus Publications.

Davis, Wade. 2009. *The Wayfinders: Why Ancient Wisdom Matters in the Modern World.* Toronto: House of Anansi Press.

Day, Allan H. 2014. *The Horse Lover: A Cowboy's Quest to Save the Wild Mustangs.* Lincoln, NE: Bison Books.

Denhardt, Robert Moorman. 1949. *The Horse of the Americas.* Norman: University of Oklahoma Press.

de Steiguer, J. Edward. 2011. *Wild Horses of the West: History and Politics of America's Mustangs.* Tucson: University of Arizona Press.

DeVoto, Bernard. 2001. *The Western Paradox.* New Haven, CT: Yale University Press.

de Waal, Frans. 2016. *Are We Smart Enough to Know How Smart Animals Are?* New York: W.W. Norton.

Dines, Lisa. 2001. *The American Mustang Guidebook: History, Behavior, and State-by-State Directions on Where to Best View America's Wild Horses.* Minocqua, WI: Willow Creek Press.

Dobie, Frank J. 2005. *The Mustangs.* Lincoln, NE: Bison Books.

Donahue, Debra. 2000. *The Western Range Revisited: Removing Livestock from Public Land to Conserve Native Biodiversity.* Norman: University of Oklahoma Press.

Eckhoff, Vickery. 2015. "Livestock Data Fills Gap in Ongoing Wild Horse Debate." Retrieved from: http://dailypitchfork.org/?p=920.

Emerson, Ralph Waldo. 1983. *Essays and Lectures.* New York: Library of America.

Engelhard, Michael. 2005. *Unbridled: The Western Horse in Fiction and Nonfiction*. Guilford, CT: Lyons Press.

Farley, Terri. 2015. *Wild at Heart: Mustangs and the Young People Fighting to Save Them*. New York: HMH Books.

Flores, Dan. 2016. *American Serengeti: The Last Big Animals of the Great Plains*. Lawrence: University of Kansas Press.

———. 1999. *The Horizontal Yellow: Nature and History in the Near Southwest*. Albuquerque: University of New Mexico Press.

———. 2001. *The Natural West: Environmental History in the Great Plains and Rocky Mountains*. Norman: University of Oklahoma Press.

Foster, Charles. 2016. *Being a Beast: Adventures Across the Species Divide*. New York: Metropolitan Books.

Fuller, Alexandra. 2009. "Mustangs: Spirit of the Shrinking West." *National Geographic*. Retrieved from: https://www.nationalgeographic.com/magazine/2009/02/wild-horses.html.

Glaser, Christine, Chuck Romaniello, and Karyn Moskowitz. 2015. *Cost and Consequences: The Real Price of Livestock Grazing on America's Public Lands*. Retrieved from: https://www.biologicaldiversity.org/programs/public_lands/grazing/pdfs/CostsAndConsequences_01-2015.pdf.

Haines, Francis. 1971. *Horses in America: The Story of American Horses and Their Riders, from Eohippus of Prehistory to the Rodeos of Today*. New York: Thomas Y. Crowell.

Harbury, Martin. 1984. *The Last of the Wild Horses*. New York: Doubleday.

Harrell Clark, LaVerne. 1966. *They Sang for Horses: The Impact of the Horse on Navajo and Apache Folklore*. Tucson: University of Arizona Press.

Harris, Moira. 2009. *Wild Horses of the World*. New York: Octopus Books.

Hartley Edward, Elwyn. 1995. *Wild Horses: A Spirit Unbroken*. Stillwater, MN: Voyageur Press.

Hausman, Gerald. 2003. *The Mythology of the Horse: Horse Legend and Lore throughout the Ages*. New York: Three Rivers Press.

Hayes, Tim. 2015. *Riding Home: The Power of Horses to Heal*. New York: St. Martin's Press.

Hogan, Linda. 2020. *The Radiant Lives of Animals*. Boston: Beacon Press.

Hoglund, Don. 2006. *Nobody's Horses: The Dramatic Rescue of the Wild Herd of White Sands*. New York: Free Press.

Howard, R. W. 1965. *The Horse in America*. New York: Follett Publishing.

Howey, M. Oldfield. 2002. *The Horse in Magic and Myth*. New York: Dover.

Hubert, Marie-Luce, and Jean-Louis Klein. 2007. *Mustangs: Wild Horses of the West*. Richmond Hill, ON: Firefly Books.

Hurwitt, Mara C. 2017. "Freedom versus Forage: Balancing Wild Horses and Livestock Grazing on the Public Lands." *Idaho Law Review*, 53(425): 426–63.

Isaacson, Rupert. 2009. *The Horse Boy: A Father's Quest to Heal His Son*. New York: Little, Brown.

James, William. 1902. *The Varieties of Religious Experience*. New York: Longmans, Green.

Kathrens, Ginger. 2017. *Cloud: Wild Stallion of the Rockies*, Revised and Updated. East Petersburg, PA: Companion House Books.

———. 2019. *Cloud's Legacy: The Wild Stallion Returns*. East Petersburg, PA: Companion House Books.

Ketcham, Christopher. 2019. *This Land: How Cowboys, Capitalism, and Corruption Are Ruining the American West*. New York: Viking.

Kirkpatrick, Jay F., and Michael H. Francis. 1994. *Into the Wind: The Wild Horses of North America*. Minocqua, WI: Northword Press.

———, and Patricia Fazio. 2005. "Wild Horses as Native North American Wildlife: A Statement of the 110th Congress." Retrieved from: http://skymountainwild.org /documents/WildHorsesasNativeNorthAmericanWildlife .pdf.

Klyza, Christopher. 1996. *Who Controls Public Lands? Mining, Forestry, and Grazing Policies 1870–1990*. Charlotte: University of North Carolina Press.

Kohanov, Linda. 2010. *The Tao of Equus: A Woman's Journey of Healing and Transformation through the Way of the Horse*. Novato, CA: New World Library.

Kolbert, Elizabeth. 2012. "Recall of the Wild: The Quest to Engineer a World before Humans." Retrieved from: https://www.newyorker.com/magazine/2012/12/24 /recall-of-the-wild.

Lane, Belden. 2007. *The Solace of Fierce Landscapes: Exploring Desert and Mountain Spirituality*. New York: Oxford University Press.

Lipka, Michael, and Claire Gecewicz. 2017. "More Americans Now Say They're Spiritual but Not Religious." Pew Research Center. Retrieved from: https://www .pewresearch.org/fact-tank/2017/09/06/more-americans -now-say-theyre-spiritual-but-not-religious/.

Lokting, Britta. 2020. "The Wild Horse Wars: In the West, Wild Horses Are an Out-of-Control Problem—and Ranchers and Animal Rights Activists Are Locked in Conflict over Their Fate." *The Washington Post*. Retrieved from: https://washingtonpost.com/magazine/2020/11/18/wild-horses-ranchers-animal-rights-activists/.

Lorenz Franzen, Jens. 2010. *The Rise of Horses: 55 Million Years of Evolution*. Baltimore, MD: Johns Hopkins University Press.

Louv, Richard. 2019. *Our Wild Calling: How Connecting with Animals Can Transform Our Lives—and Save Theirs*. Chapel Hill, NC: Algonquin Books.

Marris, Emma. 2011. *Rambunctious Garden: Saving Nature in a Post-Wild World*. New York: Bloomsbury.

Maslow, Abraham. 1964. *Religions, Values, and Peak Experiences*. Columbus: Ohio State University Press.

McKnight, Tom L. 1959. "The Feral Horse in Anglo-America." *Geographical Review*, 49(4): 506–25.

McMaster University. 2021. "Ancient DNA found in soil samples reveals mammoths, Yukon wild horses survived thousands of years longer than believed." *Newswise*. Retrieved from: https://tinyurl.com/bddkpsmk.

Merrill, Karen. 2002. *Public Lands and Political Meaning: Ranchers, the Government, and the Property between Them*. Berkeley: University of California Press.

Mills, C. Wright. 1959. *The Sociological Imagination*. New York: Oxford University Press.

Monbiot, George. 2017. *Feral: Rewilding the Land, the Sea, and Human Life*. Chicago: University of Chicago Press.

Moor, Robert. 2017. *On Trails: An Exploration*. New York: Simon & Schuster.

Morris, Desmond. 1988. *Horse Watching*. New York: Crown Publishing.

Muhn, James, and Hanson R. Stuart. 1988. *Opportunity and Challenge: The Story of the BLM.* Washington, DC: Department of the Interior, Bureau of Land Management.

Muir, John. 2012. *Wilderness Essays.* Layton, UT: Gibbs Smith.

National Research Council. 2013. "Using Science to Improve the BLM Wild Horse and Burro Program: A Way Forward." Washington, DC: The National Academies Press. https://doi.org/10.17226/13511.

Newberg, Andrew. 2021. "How an Intense Spiritual Retreat Might Change Your Brain." *Psyche.* Retrieved from: https://psyche.co/ideas/how-an-intense-spiritual-retreat -might-change-your-brain.

Olalde, Mark. 2019. "Forever Mines: Loopholes Allow Mine Companies to Avoid Cleanup Indefinitely." *High Country News,* 51(20): 24–30.

Outwater, Alice. 2019. *Wild at Heart: America's Turbulent Relationship with Nature, from Exploitation to Redemption.* New York: St. Martin's Press.

Owen, James P. 2005. *Cowboy Ethics: What Wall Street Can Learn from the Code of the West.* New York: Stoecklein Publishing.

Paskett, Parley J. 1986. *Wild Mustangs.* Logan: Utah State University Press.

Phillips, David. 2018. "Let Mountain Lions Eat Horses." *New York Times* (May 13, section SR): 9.

———. 2017. *Wild Horse Country: The History, Myth, and Future of the Mustang.* New York: W.W. Norton.

———. 2021. "Wild Horses Adopted under a Federal Program Are Going to Slaughter." *New York Times* (May 16, section A): 20.

Pomeranz, Lynne. 2006. *Among Wild Horses: A Portrait of the Pryor Mountain Mustangs.* North Adams, MA: Storey Publishing.

Popper, Deborah E., and Frank J. Popper. 2006. "The Onset
   of the Buffalo Commons." *Journal of the West.*
   45(2): 29–34.

Price, Steve. 2017. *America's Wild Horses: The History of the Western
   Mustang.* New York: Skyhorse Publishers.

Public Employees for Environmental Responsibility. 2018. "BLM's
   Livestock Program Ravages Public Lands and Rips Off the
   Taxpayer." Retrieved from: https://www.peer.org/assets
   /docs/blm/7_12_18_PEER_Grazing_Testimony.pdf.

Purdy, Jedediah. 2019. *This Land Is Our Land: The Struggle for a
   New Commonwealth.* Princeton, NJ: Princeton University
   Press.

Raulff, Ulrich. 2017. *Farewell to the Horse: A Cultural History.* New
   York: W.W. Norton.

Rifkin, Jeremy. 1992. *Beyond Beef: The Rise and Fall of Cattle
   Culture.* New York: Penguin Books.

Rivas, Mim. 2006. *Beautiful Jim Key: The Lost History of the World's
   Smartest Horse.* New York: William Morrow Paperbacks.

Roberts, Monty. 2000. *Shy Boy: The Horse That Came In from the
   Wild.* New York: Harper Perennial.

Running Horse Collin, Yvette. 2017. "The Relationship between
   the Indigenous Peoples of the Americas and the Horse:
   Deconstructing a Eurocentric Myth." PhD diss., University
   of Alaska, Fairbanks.

Ryden, Hope. 2005. *America's Last Wild Horses: The Classic Study of
   the Mustangs, Their Pivotal Role in the History of the West,
   Their Return to the Wild, and the Ongoing Efforts to Preserve
   Them.* New York: Lyons Press.

———. 1999. *Wild Horses I Have Known.* New York: Clarion
   Books.

Safina, Carl. 2015. *Beyond Words: What Animals Think and Feel.*
   New York: Henry Holt.

Scanlan, Lawrence. 1998. *Wild about Horses: Our Timeless Passion for the Horse*. New York: Perennial.

Scott, Traer. 2008. *Wild Horses: Endangered Beauty*. New York: Merrell Publishers.

Shanks, Bernard. 1984. *This Land Is Your Land: The Struggle to Save America's Public Lands*. San Francisco: Sierra Club Books.

Sheldrake, Rupert. 2018. *Science and Spiritual Practices: Transformative Experiences and Their Effects on Our Bodies, Brains, and Health*. San Francisco: Counterpoint Press.

Smith, Emily Esfahani. 2017. *The Power of Meaning: Crafting a Life That Matters*. New York: Crown.

Spragg, Mark, ed. *Thunder of the Mustangs*. New York: Sierra Club Books.

Stillman, Deanne. 2009. *Mustang: The Saga of the Wild Horse in the American West*. New York: Mariner Books.

Symanski, Richard. 1985. *Wild Horses and Sacred Cows*. Flagstaff, AZ: Northland Press.

Thompson, Ken. 2014. *Where Do Camels Belong? Why Invasive Species Aren't All Bad*. New York: Greystone Books.

Thoreau, Henry David. 2007. *Walden*. New York: Library of America.

Tippett, Krista. 2017. *Becoming Wise: An Inquiry into the Mystery and Art of Living*. New York: Penguin Books.

United States Bureau of Land Management. 2015. *Environmental Assessment: Red Desert Complex Herd Management Area Gather*. Retrieved from: DOI-BLM-WY-030-EA15-63.

Walker, Carol. 2016. *Galloping to Freedom: Saving the Adobe Town Appaloosas*. Longmont, CO: Painted Hills Publishing.

———. 2008. *Wild Hoof Beats: America's Vanishing Wild Horses*. Longmont, CO: Painted Hills Publishing.

Walker, Wyman. 1945. *The Wild Horse of the West*. Lincoln: University of Nebraska Press.

Western, Sam. *Pushed Off the Mountain, Sold Down the River: Wyoming's Search for Its Soul*. Moose, WY: Homestead Publications.

White, Curtis. 2017. *The Barbaric Heart: Faith, Money, and the Crisis of Nature*. New York: Routledge.

Williams, Florence. 2017. *The Nature Fix: Why Nature Makes Us Happier, Healthier, and More Creative*. New York: W.W. Norton.

Williams, Paige. 2016. The Remarkable Comeback of Przewalski's Horse. *Smithsonian*. Retrieved from: https://www.smithsonianmag.com/science-nature /remarkable-comeback-przewalski-horse-180961142/.

Williams, Wendy. 2015. *The Horse: The Epic History of Our Noble Companion*. New York: Scientific American—Farrar, Strauss, and Giroux.

Worster, Donald. 1994. *An Unsettled Country: Changing Landscapes in the American West*. Albuquerque: University of New Mexico Press.

———. 1992. *Under Western Skies: Nature and History in the American West*. New York: Oxford University Press.

Wuerthner, George, and Mollie Matteson (Eds.). 2002. *Welfare Ranching: The Subsidized Destruction of the American West*. San Francisco: Foundations for Deep Ecology 2.

ACKNOWLEDGMENTS

I am grateful to the editors of the following journals and magazines, who published earlier versions of chapters included here: *Prairie Schooner*, *The Plaid Horse*, *About Place*, *Nowhere Magazine*, and *The Wayfarer*. A special note of gratitude to the staff of *The Plaid Horse*. They selected "Searching for Equus" as a finalist for the Constance Wickes Prize in Creative Nonfiction.

I am also thankful to ART 3-2-1 and the Natrona County Public Library for hosting exhibits of the photographs herein; and, to the editors of *The Penn Review* and *Permafrost*. They first published two of the images that appear in this book.

I owe a great debt to Jennifer Thompson and the staff at the Nordlyset Literary Agency. At times, they showed more confidence in this project than I could muster myself. Likewise, this book is better than I could make it on my own due to the insights of Lil Copan and the keen minds at Broadleaf.

Finally, a word of thanks to the Wyoming Arts Council. During the time that I composed a portion of this work, I enjoyed the support of a creative writing fellowship, granted by the kind and dedicated people of the WAC.

This project is supported in part by an award from the Wyoming Arts Council, with funding from the Wyoming State Legislature and the National Endowment for the Arts.

ABOUT THE AUTHOR

Chad Hanson serves as a member of the faculty in Sociology and Religion at Casper College. He is co-founder of the Wyoming Mustang Institute, which works through research and advocacy to ensure healthy and stable wild horse populations on public land. Hanson is also the author of several books, including *Trout Streams of the Heart* and *This Human Shape*. He divides his time between Casper, Wyoming, and the Red Feather Lakes region of Colorado.

For more information, visit:

chadhanson.org
wyomustangs.org
instagram.com/wildhorses.wildplaces/
flickr.com/photos/124575998@N04/